"Immanuel Kant is unquestionably one of the most significant and influential figures in the history of philosophy. Summarizing and assessing his thought in a concise, accessible, and responsible fashion is no easy task, yet Alex Tseng has accomplished it. While offering his own distinctively Reformed critique of Kant's philosophical system, Tseng exemplifies scholarly integrity by challenging and correcting what he takes to be some interpretive missteps by earlier Reformed writers. The result is a fresh and thought-provoking introduction to a titan of Western philosophy."

—**James N. Anderson**, Carl W. McMurray Professor of Theology and Philosophy, Reformed Theological Seminary, Charlotte

"Immanuel Kant's influence reaches far beyond that of nineteenth-century theologians, and contemporary scholars are still considering the ways in which religion and philosophy interact in his approach. In this excellent introduction to Kant's work, Alex Tseng illuminates Kant's ideas and contributions with pertinent and broad-ranging philosophical and religious background, particularly on how Kant influenced theology as science. Even readers familiar with Kant will benefit from this fine neo-Calvinist response to one of the greatest and most influential figures in Western philosophy."

—**Annette G. Aubert**, Lecturer and Visiting Scholar of Historical Theology and Church History, Westminster Theological Seminary

"This short book packs a punch. In it, Tseng moves from historical exegesis to constructive theologizing, all the while in an accessible style, and with a clear commitment to his own branch of the Reformed tradition. For Reformed Christians looking both for a primer on Kant and for a guide to how their tradition might equip them to interact with him, this book makes a very useful contribution."

—**James Eglinton**, Meldrum Senior Lecturer in Reformed Theology, University of Edinburgh

"Kant's complex and wide-ranging philosophy shaped virtually every aspect of the modern world, and our understanding of theology and religion is no exception. Frequently hailed as the inspiration for naturalistic materialism, humanistic determinism, and much of what most Christians find wrong with the modern world, Kant is often portrayed as an enemy of the faith.

"Alex Tseng, taking his cue from recent developments in Kant interpretation, courageously exposes numerous myths about Kant that have led Christian philosophers in general and Reformed theologians in particular to reject Kant prematurely. *Immanuel Kant* offers a comprehensive yet readily accessible summary and balanced assessment of the background, key features, and primary influences of Kant's philosophy. Tseng exhibits such a refreshingly direct and straightforward style that, even if one occasionally disagrees with his conclusions, the reader is left in awe of the author's erudite scholarship and fair-minded reasoning.

"If Kant fails to provide a philosophy that Christians can fully and confidently embrace, what is the precise nature of his failure? This book offers Christians a golden opportunity to reconsider this challenging question. Just twenty-five years ago, the appearance of such a book would have been unthinkable!"

—**Stephen R. Palmquist**, Professor, Department of Religion and Philosophy, Hong Kong Baptist University

"Everything from Shao Kai Tseng is worth reading. Treating Kant neither as Christianity's bogeyman nor as its inevitable handmaiden, and in line with recent scholarship on Kant's transcendental idealism, Tseng offers a fruitful yet self-critical neo-Calvinistic engagement with the major features of Kant's philosophy. Unfailingly charitable and eminently readable."

—**Gray Sutanto**, Assistant Professor of Systematic
   Theology, Reformed Theological Seminary,
   Washington, DC

Immanuel
KANT

GREAT THINKERS

A Series

Series Editor
Nathan D. Shannon

Immanuel
KANT

Shao Kai Tseng

P&R
P U B L I S H I N G
P.O. BOX 817 • PHILLIPSBURG • NEW JERSEY 08865-0817

ISBN: 978-1-62995-701-2 (pbk)
ISBN: 978-1-62995-702-9 (ePub)
ISBN: 978-1-62995-703-6 (Mobi)

Printed in the United States of America

Library of Congress Cataloging-in-Publication Data

Names: Tseng, Shao Kai, 1981- author.
Title: Immanuel Kant / Shao Kai Tseng.
Description: Phillipsburg, New Jersey : P&R Publishing, 2020. | Series: Great thinkers | Includes index. | Summary: "Writing firmly in the Reformed tradition, Professor Shao Kai Tseng presents a reinterpretation and critical appreciation of Kant-whose complex philosophy gave rise to the secularization of modern society"-- Provided by publisher.
Identifiers: LCCN 2020011583 | ISBN 9781629957012 (paperback) | ISBN 9781629957029 (epub) | ISBN 9781629957036 (mobi)
Subjects: LCSH: Kant, Immanuel, 1724-1804.
Classification: LCC B2798 .T765 2020 | DDC 193--dc23
LC record available at https://lccn.loc.gov/2020011583

To Joanny

In Loving Memory of Aubin

CONTENTS

SERIES INTRODUCTION

Amid the rise and fall of nations and civilizations, the influence of a few great minds has been profound. Some of these remain relatively obscure even as their thought shapes our world; others have become household names. As we engage our cultural and social contexts as ambassadors and witnesses for Christ, we must identify and test against the Word those thinkers who have so singularly formed the present age.

The Great Thinkers series is designed to meet the need for critically assessing the seminal thoughts of these thinkers. Great Thinkers hosts a colorful roster of authors analyzing primary source material against a background of historical contextual issues, and providing rich theological assessment and response from a Reformed perspective.

Each author was invited to meet a threefold goal, so that each Great Thinkers volume is, first, *academically informed*. The brevity of Great Thinkers volumes sets a premium on each author's command of the subject matter and on the secondary discussions that have shaped each thinker's influence. Our authors identify the most influential features of their thinkers' work and address them with precision and insight. Second, the series maintains a high standard of *biblical and theological faithfulness*. Each volume stands on an epistemic commitment to "the whole counsel of God" (Acts 20:27), and is thereby equipped for fruitful critical engagement. Finally, Great Thinkers texts are *accessible*, not burdened with jargon or unnecessarily difficult vocabulary. The goal is to inform and equip the reader as effectively as possible through clear writing, relevant analysis, and incisive, constructive critique. My hope is that this series will distinguish itself by striking with biblical faithfulness and the riches of the Reformed tradition at the central nerves of culture, cultural history, and intellectual heritage.

Bryce Craig, president of P&R Publishing, deserves hearty thanks for his initiative and encouragement in setting the series in motion and seeing it through. Many thanks as well to P&R's director of academic development, John Hughes, who has assumed, with cool efficiency, nearly every role on the production side of each volume. The Rev. Mark Moser carried much of the burden in the initial design of the series, acquisitions, and editing of the first several volumes. And the expert participation of Amanda Martin, P&R's editorial director, was essential at every turn. I have long admired P&R Publishing's commitment, steadfast now for over eighty-five years, to publishing excellent books promoting biblical understanding and cultural awareness, especially in the area of Christian apologetics. Sincere thanks to P&R, to these fine brothers and sisters, and to several others not mentioned here for the opportunity to serve as editor of the Great Thinkers series.

Nathan D. Shannon
Seoul, Korea

FOREWORD

A handful of philosopher-theologians tower over the rest. In the ancient Asian world, it was Confucius and Laozi. In the West, we count figures such as Plato and Aristotle as foundational. Augustine, a hinge at the fall of the Roman Empire and the establishment of the Christian church, surely qualifies. Thomas Aquinas certainly qualifies. Perhaps John Calvin belongs in this company. But none in the last four hundred years matches Immanuel Kant's standing. This may seem strange, since he is very difficult to read and harder to understand. It has been said, perhaps unfairly, that to get access to most philosophers, it is best to read them in the original, whereas to fathom Kant his commentators are clearer than his own texts. Plato is a pleasure to read. Augustine may be understood by believers and unbelievers alike. Even Thomas Aquinas, whose scholastic method can be a roadblock for some, is clear, once you decipher his logic. But Kant is simply opaque.

Yet no one has influenced modern thought and theology more greatly than Kant. How can this be? It may be that philosophy as a discipline does not cause change. It can certainly be influential, and at least until recently thoughts pondered at the great universities could trickle down to the level of the ordinary person. It may be, too, though, that Kant crystallized what was happening in European culture at the end of the eighteenth century and the beginning of the nineteenth. We have become more aware of this reciprocal relationship through insights from the sociology of knowledge. As Peter Berger and others have reminded us, worldview formation is not just a one-way causal passage from ideas to social consequences. Kant thus, as the French put it, is *incontournable* ("essential" or "unavoidable").

John Frame makes the point that the greatest philosophers are not the ones who are satisfied with a narrow range of insights, but the ones "who try to bring together ideas that initially seem irreconcilable."[1] He cites Plato, who reconciled Parmenides with Heraclitus; Thomas Aquinas, who synthesized Plato, Aristotle, and Christian revelation; and, of course, Kant, who conjugated the world of the *noumenal* (*the Ding an sich*) with the world of the *phenomenal* (human experience). Frame calls this synthesis "highly creative."[2]

In the pages that follow, Shao Kai Tseng masterfully, and also highly creatively, presents the thought of Immanuel Kant and makes it accessible to the reader. He shows us how Kant, no doubt the greatest mind of the German Enlightenment, not only "opened eyes long closed but also put new blinders on them."[3] As is well known (or at least assumed), Kant defined the categories by which we tend to think of religion and science. As a good dualist, he restricted knowledge by making it rigorously scientific (pure reason) while at the same time making a place for God and

---

1. John M. Frame, *A History of Western Philosophy and Theology* (Phillipsburg, NJ: P&R Publishing, 2015), 253.

2. Frame, *History*, 253.

3. The felicitous assessment of Stephen Ozment, *A Mighty Fortress: A New History of the German People* (New York: Harper Collins, 2004), 180.

especially for morality (practical reason). Even today we tend to separate these spheres. It could be that we try to reconcile them, or even put religion to the test of science, but Kant believes that this is ultimately impossible, while yet arguing that it is better for both realms if we keep them somewhat separate.

This kind of dialectical thinking was well suited to a conservative Germany that was facing change and trying to cope with the French Revolution. But still today, many in the West agree. Or if we don't, we have perhaps become more humble, without challenging the overall scheme. Apologists who wished to verify the soul, human freedom, and even God objectively felt somehow edged out. Kant's limits were discouraging to many theologians. But not to all. Schleiermacher celebrated the emotional value of the Christian religion. And though scientists were free to pursue their work, they had to proceed without the pretension of coming of age by shaking off the church's emprise. Still, much great science was accomplished, at least some of which was made possible by protecting it from a misguided church. Succeeding philosophers would kick against these pricks, trying to consider these limits as being in need either of correction or of further development, but were never quite free of them.

For example, Johann Gottlieb Fichte claimed that he could reunify the field of vision by challenging the untouchability of Kant's *noumenal* and arguing that the human self was the ultimate reality. It wasn't going to work, since there was no real transcendence. Georg Wilhelm Friedrich Hegel believed that history was driven by the "absolute *Geist*" (Spirit). "The rational is the real and the real is the rational," Hegel claimed. But the logical conclusion of this view become a trajectory within which Nietzsche posited the *Übermensch*, which has been influential partly for good (now, we better understand the power dimension of knowledge) and partly for ill (the twentieth century witnessed the oppression of the "overman").

In their own ways, Fichte, Hegel, and many others wanted to make room for God. In the spirit of Romanticism, they sought a coexistence of humans, nature, God, and good and evil. It was not going to succeed. But it must be remembered that many in the early nineteenth century thought they were saving the Christian faith from skepticism. Most who are even slightly acquainted with Immanuel Kant recall his "Copernican revolution of thought." When Kant read David Hume, the Scottish Enlightenment philosopher, it roused him from his "dogmatic slumbers." Hume claimed to have deconstructed any rational grounds for certainty. Hume argued that there could be no verifiable assignment of causality, and thus no way to prove God as the ultimate cause. Cause is merely mental associations we make, sense impressions that cannot be measured empirically. Kant answered with his transcendental critique. If knowledge is not possible based on traditional rules of logic, are there any other principles on which it can be based? His answer was revolutionary: of course knowledge is possible, because we know! The principle is a synthetic *a priori* principle. The universe does not reveal itself to us, but we define the data received from the unknown. Almost a *what if*?

The story gets complicated, and Dr. Tseng explains it as well as anyone else. Even though you can't "get there from here," there must be a cause; otherwise, all is lost. And that cause looks very much like an absolute being who contains all perfections. One of the places that we are most likely to encounter this absolute is in ethics. But, following John Hare, Tseng says that his ethics is more de facto than de jure. Is this simply a leap of faith? At one level, it is. But the alternative, for Kant, is unthinkable. Here we are confronted with one of the great challenges of Kant studies.

Kant was brought up by a godly mother, and was strongly influenced by the pietistic pastor Albert Schultz. It would not have occurred to him that the Christian religion was not true.

He believed he was defending faith in Christ. Yet Kant's Christ is the moral ideal of humanity, not necessarily God's Son come to atone for us. Luc Ferry, the French popularizer of philosophy, says that Kant's outlook "could be described as a Christian heritage," but he adds that "that is a pure and simple secularization of certain Christian ideas."[4] Tseng ends up endorsing the Van Tillian view of Kant, but does so with a serious appreciation of Kant's quasi-Christian roots.

Coming back to our original question, why, then, is Kant so influential? Many reasons. His thought appeared to be an airtight refutation of skepticism. It seemed a great defense of science (Kant was deeply influenced by Newton). It defended traditional (*deontological*) morality. And not least, it gave us expressions such as *the sublime* to describe beautiful artwork. We can benefit from Kant's remarkable insights while eschewing the humanistic system that they ultimately espouse.

William Edgar
Professor of Apologetics
Westminster Theological Seminary
Philadelphia

4. Luc Ferry, *Kant: Une lecture des trois "Critiques"* (Paris: Grasset, 2006), 91.

ACKNOWLEDGMENTS

This book is dedicated to my friend Joanny and her late husband, Aubin. I first made an effort to wrap my mind around Kant's first *Critique* when I was an undergraduate student. I managed to understand the meaning of the term *synthetic a priori judgments* and the importance of this notion, but beyond that, I could hardly make sense of Kant's text. Then I met Joanny and Aubin. They were kind, patient, and passionate in helping me with Kant—as well as Van Til and Dooyeweerd. I stayed at their home in Glenside, Philadelphia, many times, and have always enjoyed their hospitality and friendship. Many times I prayed with them in tears and laughed with them over great food and drinks. Every conversation I had with them has turned out to be inspiring in a unique way.

Before I could finish this book, Aubin went to be with the Lord. In memory of our beloved brother, I would like to take this opportunity to acknowledge our dear friends with whom we used to enjoy fellowship together, especially Stephen and Catherine, Peter and Esther, Lyna, Pei and Steven, Easter, Gang and Grace, Henry and Li, David and Aliece, Neal, Maranatha, Ike, Tsun-En and Grace, Virginia, Mingzhi and Cindy, Dixin, and Timothy. With this group of friends, I have personally witnessed the authentic love with which Professor Edgar, Mrs. Edgar, Professor Poythress, and Mrs. Poythress of Westminster Theological Seminary have cared for Joanny and Aubin. I would also like to acknowledge all the mutual friends I have with Joanny and Aubin around the world, including the editor of this series, Nate. When Nate and I finally met in person in November 2019 at a conference in San Diego, we "clicked" right away. I am also thankful for the new friendship with Professor Stephen Palmquist that this book has occasioned. Receiving me as a brother in Christ, he went out of his way to read the manuscript with great care, and engaged with my text with detailed and often lengthy comments. I wish I had sent him my manuscript at an earlier stage, so as to have allowed for the more extensive revisions that I wish I could have made in light of his comments.

Each time I remember these names in my prayers, I feel unworthy of their friendship. Each of them has been a blessing to me and to many. I pray that I will be the same to them and to others.

1

WHY KANT MATTERS TODAY

What Has Zion to Do with Königsberg?

This is a book on the German philosopher Immanuel Kant (1724–1804). Its preliminary goal is to present an introduction to his thought on the basis of an academically up-to-date interpretation. This is to set the stage for an assessment of Kant's philosophy and his role in the history of thought from a confessionally Reformed perspective.

I freely admit that I hold to a neo-Calvinist position on matters of theology, philosophy, and ethics. As a historian of modern Christian thought, I find the dogmatics and ethics of Herman Bavinck (1854–1921) to be the most convincing articulation of confessional Reformed orthodoxy in modern times. I take the presuppositionalism of Cornelius Van Til (1895–1987) to be a coherent expression of the dogmatic system of neo-Calvinism in the area of epistemology.

Yet I also admit that I find traditional neo-Calvinist readings of Kant flawed. The interpretations found in the writings of Bavinck and Van Til, as well as Abraham Kuyper (1837–1920) and Herman Dooyeweerd (1894–1977), were shaped and informed by paradigms of philosophical studies that dominated their respective generations and geographical areas. Bavinck's misclassification of Kant as a theological agnostic, for instance, reflects the mainstream scholarly opinion of his time. Despite this shortcoming, Bavinck's assessment of Kant's philosophy is, overall, fair and insightful.

Van Til's reading of Kant, however, pertains to the dominant American paradigm of his day, and contemporary scholars generally deem it to be explicitly contradictory to what we know about Kant's texts and context. To Van Til's credit, his misinterpretation of Kant resonated with some of the most authoritative Anglophone scholars of his generation (e.g., P. F. Strawson). He should be commended for having followed the pioneers of Kant studies to the frontiers. He did not simply submit to the authority of his predecessors, such as Bavinck. Bavinck (correctly) observed that Reformed theology and Kant are in agreement on the empirical limits of human knowledge (see chapter 3), but Van Til updated himself with contemporary literature and claimed (wrongly) that Kant was an empirical skeptic (see chapter 2). Even though Van Til misinterpreted Kant, his willingness to keep his academic knowledge updated and to disagree with the masters of his own tradition exemplifies the true spirit of Reformed scholarship.

I am afraid, however, that many Reformed believers today, unlike our predecessors, simply inherit outdated misinterpretations without going back to the sources and consulting recent academic literature. I personally know a number of Van Tillians who trust Van Til's criticisms of Kant and others (most notably Karl Barth) so blindly that they do not see any need to engage with primary and secondary sources. It appears to me that this often reflects inconsistent applications or even violations of some basic principles of Reformed theology.

In this book, then, my aim is not only to offer a reinterpretation of Kant that, to the best of my ability, endeavors to allow his texts to speak for themselves from his context, while taking seriously ongoing debates in the secondary literature. I will also seek to honor some basic neo-Calvinist principles in both my interpretational methods and attitude.

Specifically, I have in mind the principles of the *antithesis* and *common grace*. The former dictates that there is no neutrality between regenerate and unregenerate reason. The two will always hold to different sets of basic presuppositions and interpret the same facts, data, and information within fundamentally diverging worldview systems. Lest this be misconstrued as a post-truth approach to public discourse, the principle of common grace serves to remind us that regenerate and unregenerate minds are creatures of God alike, and that no creature can escape God's self-revelation given in and through creation and providence. Because God's revelation is perspicuous—everywhere perspicuous—the Christian must be reminded time and again that we should never give up striving for objectivity in the process of truth-seeking in all spheres of human existence. So what are some implications of these principles for the attitudes and methods with which we might reinterpret Kant?

For readers unfamiliar with the philosopher, it may be helpful to answer this question by starting with a brief introduction to the man and his life. Kant was born in the Prussian city of Königsberg (literally "King's Mount"), present-day Kaliningrad, Russia. Historically, this small city had been a prominent university town that hosted the likes of E. T. A. Hoffmann (1776–1822) and Hannah Arendt (1906–75). Kant is known, among other anecdotal facts, for having never left his hometown during his lifetime.

In the pantheon of human wisdom, Kant is in a league where only the few brightest luminaries shine. The philosopher Alfred North Whitehead (1861–1947) once commented that "the safest general characterization of the European philosophical tradition is that it consists of a series of footnotes to Plato."[1] This rhetorical overstatement might be even less of an exaggeration if we substitute "modern philosophy" and "Kant" for "the European philosophical tradition" and "Plato," respectively. Roger Scruton, in his classic introductory volume, comments that Kant's "*Critique of Pure Reason* is the most important work of philosophy to have been written in modern times; it is also one of the most difficult."[2] There is little dispute that as far as influence is concerned, the stature of Kant in the history of Western philosophy is commensurate to that of Plato and Aristotle, paralleled in modern times by almost none, with perhaps very few exceptions such as G. W. F. Hegel (1770–1831). These philosophers represent the summit of worldly wisdom.

The ancient question of the Latin church father Tertullian (ca. 155–ca. 240), then, arises for the Christian reader: "What has Jerusalem to do with Athens, the Church with the Academy, the Christian with the heretic . . . ?"[3] Or, in the case of Kant: what has Zion, mount of the King of kings, to do with Königsberg? For Tertullian, this rather cavalier question can be raised only rhetorically, for "after Jesus we have no need of speculation, after the Gospel no need of research."[4] My hope, however, is that the reader will begin the journey of this book by considering this question in a serious manner. The way that we answer this question will determine the *attitude* that we adopt.

It should be self-evident to the reader that Tertullian's Jerusalem-Athens dualism is fundamentally incompatible with any worldview that may properly be called Reformed. Yet it has

1. Alfred North Whitehead, *Process and Reality* (New York: Free Press, 1979), 39.
2. Roger Scruton, *Kant* (Oxford: Oxford University Press, 1982), 11.
3. Tertullian, *Prescription against Heretics*, in *Ante-Nicene Fathers*, ed. Alexander Roberts and James Donaldson, vol. 3 (Peabody, MA: Hendrickson, 1994), 249.
4. Tertullian, *Prescription against Heretics*, 249.

often been the case that conservative Reformed believers—some of them renowned scholars—would fall into the temptation of treating non-Christian philosophies with simplistic friend-or-foe mindsets. Kant, Hegel, and Schleiermacher have often been feared and hated in conservative Reformed circles as the modern archenemies of Christianity; believers have often been cautioned against any positive appreciation of their philosophies, however critical such appreciations may be. Such antagonism, I am afraid, is dogmatically contradictory to the Reformed faith, and is not an attitude that the finest Reformed minds in history—Witsius, Edwards, Hodge, Kuyper, Bavinck, to name but a few—have adopted.

In my interpretation and appraisal of Kant's thought, I will adopt a neo-Calvinist philosophy of revelation, with Bavinck as my chief guide.[5] This carries at least three implications. First, I will endeavor to imitate the kind of Reformed charity and "eclecticism" that Bavinck (as well as Kuyper and Hodge, among others) exemplifies.[6] Second, both the appreciative and critical aspects of my assessments will be regulated by my commitment

5. See Herman Bavinck, *Philosophy of Revelation*, ed. Cory Brock and Nathaniel Gray Sutanto (Peabody, MA: Hendrickson, 2019).

6. The term *eclecticism* has been recently highlighted by Cory Brock and Nathaniel Gray Sutanto, "Herman Bavinck's Reformed Eclecticism: On Catholicity, Consciousness, and Theological Epistemology," *Scottish Journal of Theology* 70, 3 (2017): 310–32. It is a term that emerges in the writings of the neo-Calvinist masters. My reading of Bavinck is in line with what has recently come to be called the *Edinburgh school*. The interpretational trajectory was initiated by James Eglinton, *Trinity and Organism: Towards a New Reading of Herman Bavinck's Organic Motif* (London: Bloomsbury, 2012). It has been further developed by Dr. Eglinton's former and current doctoral students, including Brock and Sutanto. This interpretation is set against an older paradigm known as the *two Bavincks hypothesis*, which posits fundamental contradictions in the writings of Bavinck between his confessional orthodoxy and his occasionally positive uses of German idealism. Underlying this hypothesis is a kind of spiritual separatism akin to that of Tertullian, which dominated the theological seminary in Kampen, where Bavinck once taught. It must be clarified, however, that Professor Jan Veenhof, the leading figure of this interpretational paradigm, stands firmly against the nature-grace dualism of which Tertullian is representative. See Jan Veenhof, *Revelatie en Inspiratie* (Amsterdam: Buijten & Schipperheijin, 1968).

to Reformed orthodoxy, delimited by the historic confessional standards, which I, following Bavinck, take to be the basic framework of a consistently Christian worldview. Third, I will interact with and learn from secular academia, not as an outsider, but as a member of the academic community, which I understand to be a social sphere instituted by God's common-grace design.

Toward an Objective Criticism

The third point above raises a question relating to the *method* of interpretation. Because this book seeks to offer a criticism of Kant's thought, our assessment has to be based on an objective interpretation. Precisely because we need to strive for objectivity, we cannot remain neutral in our presentation of Kant's philosophy. The problem is that interpretation of even the most fundamental doctrine in Kant's philosophy (called *transcendental idealism*) remains controversial today. How can I claim to be objective in my reading if there is no neutrality among even the most authoritative Kant scholars of our day?

This question arises only if one confuses *objectivity* with *neutrality*, which are obviously different concepts. In a court of law, for example, there is no neutrality between defense and prosecution, but this does not alleviate the need for the judge and jury to strive for objectivity in the verdict. Yet the difficulty remains: when even the best interpreters in the field have not been able to reach a final consensus, how can we determine which side of the debate is most objective?

The good news is that we are not required to play the presumptuous role of judge or jury in this case. Leading scholars in the field today generally make easily recognizable in their writings the various assumptions to which they hold, as well as the various interpretational emphases that they place on text, context, and contemporary reader responses. This means that the task of recognizing an interpretational model that is most objective will not be hopelessly subjective: we will choose a model that consciously seeks to honor the text and the context as comprehensively as possible. This method of interpretation, as far as I can see, is the only approach that accords with biblical ethics, if we take seriously our Lord's command not to judge.[7]

Next, we need to consider how to deal with inconsistencies in Kant's thought. No serious interpreter, however charitable, will deny that there are inconsistencies in Kant's arguments, some of which can be quite radical. We must nonetheless acknowledge the fact that when he came to be aware of his own inconsistencies, he was, more often than not, quite ready to modify his own position, sometimes in ad hoc manners, but sometimes in more fundamental ways. Thus, we must not be too harsh when we spot an argument or premise that is inconsistent with his express intentionality or his most fundamental set of assumptions.

As critical readers, we are, of course, warranted and required to "read between the lines"—to look for hidden assumptions. But whenever Kant makes his assumptions explicit, we should exercise restraint in attributing to him contradictory assumptions that he rejects, unless we have firm evidence that he is contradicting himself. When a text can entail different assumptions that he does not spell out, we should not read into the text any assumption that is inconsistent with his fundamental presuppositions, with the context, and with his overall philosophical framework. We should, in principle, avoid any friend-or-foe mindset before allowing Kant's texts to speak for themselves from his

7. I will be forthright in identifying the basic approach presented by Karl Ameriks as the one that I adopt. I do not claim that his model is necessarily or entirely correct. I take issue especially with how he habitually uses the word *faith* as something mysterious and nonrational. Yet we can at least acknowledge that he consciously strives for objectivity by honoring both text and context in the most comprehensive way. I have also been significantly influenced by Henry Allison's model, though I think some of his views are reconcilable to those of his opponents.

context. The doctrine of total depravity does not warrant anyone to be above the law and disregard the presumption of innocence—be it in a court of law, in everyday encounters, or in the critical appraisal of a philosopher's thought.

Finally, if we follow our neo-Calvinist masters in believing that ultimate consistency cannot be attained in unbiblical systems of thought, then we are forbidden to think that any unbiblical philosophy can consistently oppose God's truth in all its assertions. Kant was in fact so deeply informed by his religious upbringing that many aspects of his philosophy can be aligned with Christian doctrine in formal ways.[8]

I will take my cue from Professor John Hare and interpret Kant's project as an attempt to translate traditional Christian doctrine into a philosophy and religion of pure reason. Partly relying on Professor Hare, I will argue that this project fails at two pivotal points, the first methodological and the second substantive. These are (1) Kant's severance of faith from knowledge, and (2) his attempt to answer the question of hope by tackling the problem of the atonement. Although I see these as two planks on which the whole edifice of Kantian philosophy stands or falls (here I am more critical of Kant than Professor Hare), I will suggest that the building blocks of Kant's thought can prove invaluable to our reflections on God and his ways, if we are able to eclectically incorporate them into our own system.

Kant's Continuing Significance

Kant's works are notoriously difficult. He invented some peculiar terms, and many of them do not carry unified definitions throughout his writings. His three famous *Critiques*, often

---

8. In this respect, I have been inspired for the most part by the writings of Professor John Hare and Professor Stephen Palmquist.

referred to as his *Critical works*, are among the most frequently mentioned philosophical opuses of all time. These are the *Critique of Pure Reason* (1781 and 1787), the *Critique of Practical Reason* (1788), and the *Critique of the Power of Judgment* (1790). Notwithstanding their preeminence, they are in fact seldom read in entirety, even within the field of academic philosophy. In the parts of the world where I have studied and taught—North America, the UK, Taiwan, and mainland China—the majority of undergraduate students in philosophy encounter Kant's thought only through textbooks and lectures.

One reason why Kant's famous works are read by only a small minority even in academic philosophy has to do with their difficulty. Unlike nineteenth-century philosophers such as Hegel, Schleiermacher, Kierkegaard, Nietzsche, Schopenhauer, and others who wrote in more historical-narrative, didactic, literary, or even poetic styles, Kant's works were uncompromisingly scholastic. The problem is that the complexity and sophistication of his scholastic writings were elevated to a level hitherto unseen in the history of philosophy.

Philosophers of Kant's own day quickly recognized the significance of his Critical philosophy upon the publication of the first edition of his *Critique of Pure Reason* ("first *Critique*"), but the majority of them found the work unapproachable without the aid of a popular interpreter such as Karl Leonhard Reinhold (1757–1825). As Karl Ameriks puts it, "the first edition of the *Critique* in 1781 was the major intellectual event of its day, but it completely perplexed even its best-prepared readers—until the appearance in 1786–87 of Reinhold's *Letters on the Kantian Philosophy*."[9]

Another reason why Kant has been ignored by so many

---

9. Karl Ameriks, *Kant and the Historical Turn: Philosophy as Critical Interpretation* (Oxford: Oxford University Press, 2006), 7.

academic philosophers today has to do with the ways in which they understand the task of philosophy. Interestingly, this is a case in which a philosopher seems to have dug his own grave. Philosophy after Kant underwent convoluted developments down to our own day, but the overall trend has been that philosophers increasingly understood their task to be *interpretive*, rather than *speculative*. Philosophers of our day generally prefer to focus on tangible phenomena, rather than to speculate about the big ideas with which Kant himself was concerned—God, freedom, immortality, the world, the soul, morality, religion, and so on.

Paradoxically, this very reason for which philosophers moved away from Kant has also drawn them back to Kant in recent decades. Recent philosophy seeks to focus on interpreting how people concretely live, think, speak, and write within specific cultural-historical contexts. By doing so, philosophers have discovered that these interpretive tasks are impossible if we fail to appreciate Kant's influence. Hardly any sphere of modern reality is not overshadowed—sometimes even indoctrinated—by Kant.

It may serve well to demonstrate this point by beginning with an anecdote of my own. In my volume on Hegel in the present series, I talked about how Kant (and Hegel) introduced me to Calvin, as it were. But Kant was also a key figure at another important juncture in my life. That was when I first met my wife, Jasmine.

I offered a course on systematic theology for lay church leaders in Asia, and Jasmine attended. I demonstrated a specific point with the paintings of Rembrandt, and she approached me after class to discuss matters of theology and the arts. I learned that she was a fashion designer with solid background in the fine arts and art history, both European and Chinese. We became so impassioned in these conversations that they were eventually carried over to email and social media after I returned to the UK for doctoral studies.

A decisive breakthrough in our relationship came at a point when Kant was mentioned in our discussions. She asked me how the influence of Christianity has made European art different from Oriental art. In response, I brought up Kant's notion of *the sublime.*

"But Kant's notion of the sublime is fundamentally different from any truly Christian understanding of God's glory or transcendence," Jasmine replied.

Then I fell in love with her. To be more precise, I began to allow myself to "follow my heart," as it were—but that is not the point here. As we continued our conversation, I became curious about her grasp of the Kantian notion of the sublime.

"I read it in an art history textbook. It's something that all students of art history must know," she told me.

This is an instance of the extent of Kant's influence. No modern theory of art can escape discussions of the beautiful and the sublime. Kant was, of course, not the first philosopher to employ these terms: his early, pre-Critical work on this subject simply addressed a topic of ongoing scholarly debates.[10] But the way in which he delimits these notions in the *Critique of the Power of Judgment* has set a standard for subsequent theories of art.

Some have concurred with Kant that art can convey only the beautiful, but not the sublime. The immediately ensuing generation, however, tended to see Kant's delimitations of the beautiful and the sublime as an impasse to be overcome. The way in which Friedrich Schiller (1759–1805) wrestled with Kant, for instance, became a source of inspiration for nineteenth-century romanticism, which reacted against Kant by attempting to show that the artist can indeed creatively represent not only the beautiful but also the sublime in tangible ways. Depictions of the natural

10. Immanuel Kant, *Bemerkungen in den Beobachtungen über das Gefühl des Schönen und Erhabenen*, ed. Marie Rischmüller (Hamburg: Felix Meiner Verlag, 1991).

sublime in the paintings of the German artist Caspar David Friedrich (1774–1840) and the sublimity of human nature in dramatic tragedy expressed by the unique tonality of the operatic compositions of Richard Wagner (1813–83) are well-known examples. The Anglophone reader might be more familiar with literary imaginations of the sublime in the poetry of William Wordsworth (1770–1850) and Samuel Taylor Coleridge (1772–1834). The trend in twentieth- and twenty-first-century art and art theory has been, by and large, to treat the beautiful and the sublime as entirely subjective feelings in the observer that have nothing to do with the object being observed. C. S. Lewis famously defended the objectivity of the sublime in his 1934 *Abolition of Man* against this trend by discussing "the well-known story of Coleridge at the waterfall."[11]

Whatever position one takes in the debates on the beautiful and the sublime, Kant is usually understood as one who set the rules of the game, as it were. Even if he is not always mentioned or engaged with directly, no aesthetic theory after him has been able to completely bypass him. Art and music as we know them today would have indeed been very different without the influence of Kant.

Another Kantian notion globally influential today, closely related to those of the beautiful and the sublime, is that of human dignity. As Christopher McCrudden, world-renowned expert on human-rights law, Fellow of the British Academy no less, puts it, "The concept of human dignity has probably never been so omnipresent in everyday speech, or so deeply embedded in political and legal discourse."[12]

Again, just as Kant did not create the notions of the beautiful

---

11. C. S. Lewis, *The Abolition of Man* (New York: HarperCollins, 1974), 1–5.

12. Christopher McCrudden, "In Pursuit of Human Dignity: An Introduction to Current Debates," in *Understanding Human Dignity*, ed. Christopher McCrudden (Oxford: Oxford University Press, 2013), 1.

and the sublime *ex nihilo*, he was not the first person to use the term *dignity* with definitions familiar to us in sociopolitical discourses today. Professor Michael Rosen neatly summarizes the contemporary definition of the term as "an 'inner, transcendental kernel'—something intangible that all human beings carry inalienably inside them that underlies the moral claims that they have just by being human."[13] Kant is usually credited with having solidified this basic definition of *dignity*. It is true, as a recent volume on the history of dignity has shown, that Kant did not "construct his argument for dignity out of whole cloth," and that there were "earlier innovators of the modern concept."[14] Yet even though "Kant's fame in this matter" may not be "fully deserved . . . , there *is* something revolutionary in Kant's thought . . . in the way Kant justifies the requirement to respect all others."[15]

As a final example of Kant's continuing relevance in contemporary society, let us consider our conception of science in the modern world. In English, *science* often refers specifically to the natural sciences. Its Latin origin, *scientia*, from *scire* ("to know"), however, refers to systems of demonstrable knowledge. The German word for *science* is *Wissenschaft*, formed by *wissen* ("to know") and the suffix *-schaft* (etymologically related and close in meaning to the English suffix *-ship*). Any academic discipline with a well-defined set of methods to demonstrate what it claims to know about its object of inquiry is properly called a *science*.

Kant lived in a time when the radical developments of how Europeans conceptualized their knowledge of the world were

13. Michael Rosen, *Dignity: Its History and Meaning* (Cambridge, MA: Harvard University Press, 2014), 9.

14. Remy Debes, "Introduction," in *Dignity: A History*, ed. Remy Debes (Oxford: Oxford University Press, 2017), 3–4.

15. Oliver Sensen, "Dignity: Kant's Revolutionary Conception," in *Dignity: A History*, 238 (italics original).

often likened to a revolution (though the term *scientific revolution* was not coined until the twentieth century). The overwhelming success of Newtonian physics led many of Kant's contemporaries to consider Isaac Newton's publication of the *Philosophiæ Naturalis Principia Mathematica* in 1687 as the inauguration of the final phase of the revolution of human knowledge. Kant himself saw Newtonian physics as a paradigmatic example of *Wissenschaft*. His task as a philosopher was to reconceptualize what we call *science*, that is, what we claim to *know* by means of conceptual theorization and empirical observation.

We will reserve the details of Kant's theses and arguments for the next chapter. Suffice it now to say that in Kant's system, our knowledge is drastically limited to the domain of nature, which is immanent to our cognitive faculties. While Kant's intention was to preserve morality and religion in the wake of the scientific revolution, the net result of his Critical philosophy has been an increasingly naturalistic view of science that denies the scientific status of traditional theology.

It is important to make distinctions when we apply such labels as *naturalism* and *idealism* to Kant. He is not a naturalist or even a deist with regard to revelation, but his view of science is certainly naturalistic. This has to do with the way in which he is an empirical realist and transcendental idealist in the theoretical use of reason, and a transcendental realist in the practical use of reason (see chapter 2).

Kant's limitation of knowledge to the realm of the natural has had a significant bearing on various views of science in recent history down to our own day. Even a philosopher as averse to the Kantian system as Bertrand Russell, for instance, would retain the view that definite knowledge pertains to science, which inquires only into tangible things. Russell rebelled against the Kantian system by rejecting what he (mis)understood to be Kantian idealism, but that was only to carry through with the naturalistic impulse of Kant's view of science. A famous quote from Russell's celebrated *History of Western Philosophy* reflects a widely accepted view of science and "definite knowledge" in the modern era that is in many ways derived from Kant:

> Philosophy, as I shall understand the word, is something inter-mediate between theology and science. Like theology, it con-sists of speculations on matters as to which definite knowledge has, so far, been unascertainable; but like science, it appeals to human reason rather than to authority, whether that of tradi-tion or that of revelation. All *definite* knowledge—so I should contend—belongs to science; all *dogma* as to what surpasses definite knowledge belongs to theology. But between theology and science there is a No Man's Land, exposed to attack from both sides; this No Man's Land is philosophy.[16]

Kant's dominance in modern views of science has given rise to one of the deepest questions driving the developments of modern theology: how can theology be a science? In one sense, the whole of modern Protestant (and, to a lesser but also sig-nificant extent, Catholic) theology—orthodox or not—stands under the shadow of Kant. This is certainly an important reason why Christian readers should give Kant a read.

In the third chapter of this book, we will offer an overview of Kant's influence on modern theology. We will then rely on historic Reformed theology and neo-Calvinism to construe a Christian understanding of science and knowledge. I do not intend to offer a theory strictly associated with any Reformed thinker. My hope is to be as catholic as I can within the bounds of confessional Reformed theology, so as to offer the average

---

16. Bertrand Russell, *History of Western Philosophy* (London: Routledge, 2004), xiii (italics added).

Reformed reader a basic worldview with which to hold on to the faith as a "firm and certain knowledge" (Calvin) in an age in which academic learning at all levels, despite increasing cultural superstitions in broader society, is still dominated by naturalistic paradigms.

2

A SUMMARY OF
KANT'S THOUGHT

Kant's Thought in Context

Early-Modern Rationalism

In lieu of a personal biography, which is readily available
from trustworthy sources on the Internet anyway, let us begin
with an introduction to the intellectual-historical context of
Kant's thought. René Descartes (1596–1650) is often considered the founder of early-modern philosophy, and few historians
of thought today would contest the view that Kant stands as the
great watershed figure between early-modern and modern philosophy. Accordingly, in this chapter and the next, I will present the
Cartesian and Kantian programs as two contrasting paradigms
of human knowing.

Descartes's revolutionary approach to philosophy is often
called his *method of doubt,* or *methodological skepticism.* He ten-
tatively rejects all truth claims for which doubt cannot be elimi-
nated, in order to rebuild a system of knowledge on the basis of

a proposition that the human mind can immediately ascertain with absolute rational certainty.

There is no immediate way for me, Descartes claims, to confirm that my sensory perception of the world is not mentally fabricated in some way. All I have are ideas of things in the world. The only thing I know for sure is that I am thinking and doubting. Because I cannot doubt that I am doubting, and because my doubting presupposes a doubting subject, I know for sure that I exist. Hence Descartes's famous statement, "I think, therefore I am" (*cogito, ergo sum*).

Descartes recognizes that his rational certainty about his own existence does not immediately guarantee to him that the world he perceives is real. Thus, he finds it necessary to introduce the idea of God. He offers a so-called ontological proof of God's existence. Think of a perfect being, says Descartes. It is an idea innate to all human minds, and we call it *God*. God is, by conceptual definition, perfect in all his attributes. Now, consider *existence* as an attribute. Either God possesses existence or he does not. The notion of a perfect being with all the attributes of goodness but lacking in existence is less perfect than that of a perfect being who possesses existence. *Less perfect*, however, is as good as *imperfect*: existence is a necessary condition for perfection. The notion of a perfect being that does not exist, then, is the notion of a perfect being that is imperfect. This notion, however, amounts to a conceptual self-contradiction in my mind, just like a triangle without angles. But because I am a rational being from whose mind conceptual contradictions must be expelled, I can be certain that my idea of God as a perfect being corresponds to a being that exists in reality. On the basis of rational certainty of God's perfections and existence, Descartes proceeds to argue that I can ascertain the reality of the sensory world because its Creator who endowed me with the senses is a perfect being who does not deceive.

It is important for the reader to become familiar with the passage above on Descartes because in many respects, it was this reigning Cartesian paradigm that Kant sought to topple. At the core of his Critical philosophy is the claim that the naked reason of Descartes's *ego* gives rise to a putative God's-eye view of the world and of God himself that is ultimately illusionary. "I think, therefore I am" is sophistic: "I think" already presupposes "I am," and the "therefore" is subtly deceptive. Descartes's faith in the thinking *ego* is thus blind. In the *Critique of Pure Reason*, Kant offers a famous refutation of Descartes's ontological argument by attacking its formal aspect. More fundamentally, however, Kant points out that the whole of rationalist metaphysics is doomed to fail, for it is built on the quicksand of blind faith in the thinking *ego*.

Rationalism after Descartes capitalizes on his claim that the rationality of the human mind necessitates the existence of God and the world. Kant's Critical philosophy operates on the opposite assumption, which can be spelled out in three parts: (1) naked human reason does not have the powers to ascertain that *God is*; (2) human reason can be assured that *God ought to be*, and this assurance is strengthened by divine revelation; (3) human knowledge of the world does not have its starting point in the Cartesian *ego*, but rather involves a discursive interplay between experience and the intellect. This discursivity precludes any putative God's-eye view of things. Kant's critique of human knowledge as such serves to leave room for faith, and this theological impulse underlies the whole of his Critical philosophy from the first *Critique* onward.

In the early-modern period of philosophy, Descartes's rationalist spirit culminated in the German philosophers Gottfried Wilhelm Leibniz (1646–1716) and Christian Wolff (1679–1750). The latter is especially important for understanding Kant because by his generation, Wolffian dogmas had become preeminent throughout German academia. In his early career, Kant wrote and taught in the Wolffian tradition, though he never fully embraced the ideals of the Enlightenment even during this period.

For Wolff, human reason was sufficient, and divine revelation was as obscure and redundant as Leibniz's doctrine of *monads* (whatever these are). The result of Wolff's endeavor was a more comprehensive system of philosophical dogmas founded on the basic principles of Leibnizian philosophy. Most notable are the distinctively Leibnizian principles of (1) *sufficient reason*—that behind every existence, event, or truth there must be a reason as its sufficient condition; (2) *optimism*—that God always chooses the best of all possible things; and (3) *plenitude*—that the best possible world is one in which all rational possibilities are actualized.

A true polymath, Wolff was acquainted with Chinese philosophy when sinology was not yet an academic discipline. He was especially impressed by the moral teachings of Confucius. Confucius was, for Wolff, a prime example of how human beings can possess knowledge of God's moral truths without divine revelation. Needless to say, theologians of Wolff's time—especially his Lutheran pietist colleagues at the University of Halle—were deeply troubled by his rationalism.

Wolff's faith in the powers of human reason was not restricted to the realm of moral truths. He was confident in the capacity of human reason to reduce the whole of reality to the form of syllogisms and mathematics. His dogmatic system, inspired by Leibnizian metaphysics, is sometimes called a *philosophy of possibles*: "the business of philosophy," as he puts it, "is to assign the reason of the possibility of all things."[1] All possible beings

---

1. Christian Wolff, *Logic, or Rational Thoughts on the Powers of the Human Understanding; with Their Use and Application in the Knowledge and Search of Truth*, trans. anonymous (London: L. Hawes, W. Clarke, and R. Collins, 1770), 5.

come into actual existence by definite causes, but if human reason is capable of exhausting the reason of all possible beings,
then "[among] possible things, we must admit of one necessary,
self-existent Being, otherwise something would be possible, of
which no sufficient reason could be assigned."[2]

In the spirit of Descartes, Wolff was confident that human
reason necessitates the existence of God. His proofs of God's existence are in fact repetitions of Aristotle's cosmological argument
and Descartes's ontological argument, seasoned with Leibnizian
flavors. In the language of classical metaphysics, the cosmological family of arguments pertains to *a posteriori* proofs—logical
demonstrations from effects to cause. Ontological arguments
are called *a priori*: they are logical demonstrations from cause to
effects. These terms (later to be redefined by Hume and Kant)
and their respective forms of logical demonstrations are retained
in Wolff's philosophical discourses on God and everything that
is not God.

So strong was Wolff's confidence in the comprehensive powers of human reason to exhaust all of reality that his published
writings ambitiously encompassed almost every academic subject
of his time. The pinnacle of human knowledge, of course, is still
knowledge of God. Theology for Wolff, however, is no longer an
autonomous discipline, but rather the highest subdiscipline of
metaphysics. He distinguishes between general and special metaphysics. The former is ontology, that is, the study of the notion
of *being*. The latter is divided into rational psychology (study of
the soul), rational cosmology (study of the world), and rational
theology (study of God). Whereas Leibniz admired scholastic
theologians such as Francisco Suárez (1548–1617) and agreed
with them that rationalist theology is merely complementary to
revealed theology, Wolff deemed the latter obscure and redundant.

2. Wolff, *Logic*, 5.

Wolff's rationalist system effectively amounts to no less than what Henry Allison, one of the most authoritative voices in contemporary Kant studies, calls a "putative . . . God's-eye view of things."[3] Human reason is capable of knowing all possible things as God knows them. Even more, human reason has the power to know God as God knows himself. This was what Kant found deeply troubling. Kant's critique of knowledge and dismissal of rational theology was not intended—whatever consequences it might have brought—to be an attack on traditional Christianity. It was intended, instead, to limit the theoretical use of reason to immanent realities, and to stress that we do not possess the cognitive powers to attain to any quasi-divine knowledge.

Kant's severance of faith from knowledge can be appreciated in this light as an attempt to cut off all Cartesian-Wolffian speculation about God, the world, and the self that finds the starting point of its faith-seeking-understanding project in the supposedly quasi-divine powers of human cognition. Despite his break with the early-modern rationalist tradition and his rejection of Wolff's rational psychology, cosmology, and theology, however, Kant still retained the rationalist view that the necessary truths of reason cannot be demonstrated by the contingent truths of history. This means, for both the early (Wolffian) and the mature (Critical) Kant, that even if the historical reports of revealed religions are true, they cannot be the essence of pure, moral religion. Whereas Leibniz still reserved a place for revealed theology in his rationalist program, then, Kant effectively announced with Wolff the exile of revealed theology from the realm of the sciences. To be sure, Kant had a high view of revealed theology and believed that it was compatible with pure religion, but he made it explicit that theology did not pertain to the scientific enterprise.

3. See Henry Allison, *Kant's Transcendental Idealism: An Interpretation and Defense* (New Haven, CT: Yale University Press, 2004), xvi–xvii.

Early-Modern Empiricism

One crucial factor leading to Kant's abandonment of the Wolffian paradigm and development of his Critical philosophy was his serious consideration of British empiricism that culminated in the Scottish philosopher David Hume (1711–76). Two years after the publication of the first edition of the first *Critique*, Kant famously stated in the 1783 *Prolegomena to Any Future Metaphysics*:

> I freely admit that it was the remembrance [*Erinnerung*] of David Hume which, many years ago, first interrupted my dogmatic slumber and gave my investigations in the field of speculative philosophy a completely different direction.[4]

The trustworthiness of Kant's interpretation of Hume is a topic of some debate. Because our purpose is to introduce Kant's philosophy, we will present Hume's thought in a way that accords with Kant's understanding, which may or may not do Hume justice. In fact, Kant's treatment of Hume's problem has also been subjected to intense debate, something that we must presently consider. We will proceed here by introducing the British philosophers John Locke, George Berkeley, and Hume as representing three possible ways of dealing with experience and ideas, in order to pin down the precise point of disagreement between Kant and Hume.

Early-modern empiricist treatments of experience and ideas

---

4. Immanuel Kant, *Prolegomena to Any Future Metaphysics*, ed. and trans. Gary Hatfield (Cambridge: Cambridge University Press, 2004), 10. As the editor indicates in footnote 9, "*Erinnerung* can mean a 'memory' or 'remembrance' . . . , or it can mean a 'reminder,' 'admonition,' or 'warning.'" The equivocity of the word has led to scholarly debates over when and how Kant began to develop the Critical system that came to be synonymous with his name in response to Hume's challenges. See Manfred Kuehn, "Kant's Conception of 'Hume's Problem,'" *Journal of the History of Philosophy* 21, 2 (1983): 175–94.

began as a reaction against rationalism. Descartes distinguished between three kinds of ideas: *adventitious, fictitious,* and *innate.* No rationalist in the early-modern tradition would deny that some—if not most—of our ideas come from experience. The ideas that come to our minds through the senses are described by the rationalists as *adventitious,* which means "coming from outside." There are also ideas fabricated by our minds, which Descartes calls *fictitious ideas.*

Crucial to the rationalist tradition is the *innate-ideas thesis.* Ideas such as God are innate to the human mind. That these ideas correspond to reality outside our minds can be analytically demonstrated without having to appeal to experience or matters of fact. Innate ideas as such are neither adventitious (learned through experience) nor fictitious (fabricated by psychological processes).

Descartes's understanding of innate ideas came under severe attack in 1689, when John Locke (1632–1704) published the epochal *Essay concerning Human Understanding.*[5] Often considered a founder of British empiricism, Locke launches his revolutionary attempt in book 1 of the *Essay,* which comprises refutations of the rationalist notion of innate ideas. His groundbreaking view gave rise to a new philosophical tradition known as *tabula rasa empiricism.*

Tabula rasa, meaning "blank slate," is a description of the human mind at birth: it is completely blank. All ideas are inscribed onto the mind through experience. Ideas themselves do not constitute knowledge. Knowledge is attained by the association of ideas, which is necessarily carried out by our minds as an innate function. No idea, however, is innate to the mind.

All our ideas arise from sensation and reflection. *Sensation*

---

5. See John Locke, *An Essay concerning Human Understanding* (Indianapolis: Hackett, 1996), 4–32.

refers to the reception of sensory data that affect the state of the mind, while *reflection* is the active process by which more complex ideas are produced when the mind operates on the simpler ideas gained through sensation. The qualities of material objects have the power to act on our senses to produce ideas in our minds. Our mental faculty of understanding then makes associations between ideas to give rise to knowledge. All that we can perceive and know, per Locke, are the qualities of things that come to our minds through the senses.

Because our minds are passive in the reception of sensory data, we know that there must be substances behind the qualities of things that we perceive. These substances in themselves, however, are beyond the reach of experience. In this way, Locke imposes a very critical limit on what we can and cannot know.

Locke is often described as an *empirical realist*, which is to say that he posits the existence of material substances external to our minds in such a way that our perception of the qualities of things somehow corresponds to the real substances behind them. Kant, I will contend, should also be interpreted along the lines of empirical realism. Kant fundamentally disagrees with Locke, however, in that Locke is a *transcendental realist* and Kant is a *transcendental idealist* (these intimidating terms will be explained later) in the theoretical use of reason. As Kant sees it, transcendental realism ultimately leads to empirical idealism, which is basically what we see in the developments of empiricism after Locke.

Interestingly, some have suggested that, contrary to his own intentions, Kant's transcendental idealism in fact leads also to *empirical idealism*. This account of his doctrine of transcendental idealism is based on a "phenomenalistic, essentially Berkeleian, account of what is actually experienced by the mind."[6] George Berkeley

6. Allison, *Kant's Transcendental Idealism*, 4.

(1685–1753), an Irish Anglican bishop after whom Berkeley, California, is named, offered a more thoroughgoing empiricism by removing from Locke's system a fundamentally rationalist element. In philosophy, this element is commonly known as the *Cartesian dualism* between the mind and external substances, or the cognizant subject and cognized objects. We can see from our account of Locke above that he still posits with Descartes the reality of both the subject and the object of cognition.

The basic tenet of empiricism, however, is that no idea or knowledge is possible apart from experience. If Locke is right that substances or (in Kantian language) things in themselves are beyond the reach of experience, then this empiricist doctrine would dictate that there is no way for us to know of their existence. As Berkeley followed through with Locke's empiricism, then, he came up with the famous dictum *Esse est percipi* (*aut percipere*): "To be is to be perceived (and to perceive)."

What we have immediate access to, according to Berkeley, are in fact *ideas* of things formed in our minds—and here Berkeley remains in line with the Cartesian-Lockean theory of ideas. But if this is true, and if existence is equated to perceiving and being perceived, then all that truly exist are our minds that perceive and the ideas perceived by our minds. There are no material objects above or behind our ideas of things. To be sure, Berkeley does not deny the reality of the external world: it is real because and so long as it is perceived. What he denies, instead, is the existence of corporeal substances above and behind our ideas of things. This translates to the peculiar view that nothing exists apart from one's mental perception, a doctrine known as *immaterialism* or *subjective idealism*.

Incidentally, it was popular among mid-twentieth-century scholars to interpret Kant along Berkeleian lines. The influential P. F. Strawson, for instance, defines Kant's transcendental idealism as the "doctrine . . . that reality is supersensible and that we can have no knowledge of it."[7] Accordingly, all ideas are originated by the mind. While this approach "effectively engaged central issues in contemporary . . . philosophy," Karl Ameriks warns that its central arguments were "connected only loosely to the original text."[8]

The Reformed reader should be alerted here that Cornelius Van Til lived in a time when this approach to Kant was overwhelmingly popular in American academia. It should hardly be surprising that against this intellectual background, Van Til would label Kant's philosophy as "subjectivist."[9] Van Til should be applauded for his (mis)interpretation of Kant, for it echoed the most advanced literature of his time. If we are to learn from Van Til's engagement with contemporary scholarship, however, we should heed the authoritative scholarly voices of our own day. Ameriks cautions us that mid-twentieth-century scholars' "focus on rigor and current issues came with the cost of leaving most of the original context of Kant's work out of sight."[10]

To grasp the original context of Kant's work, we must turn to Hume. The Berkeleian position, "to be is to be perceived," is retained in the Humean system. Hume, however, rejected Berkeley's view that "to perceive" (*percipere*) also translates to "to exist." That is, Hume not only denied with Berkeley the existence

---

7. Peter Strawson, *The Bounds of Sense: An Essay on Kant's* Critique of Pure Reason (London: Routledge, 1975), 38. The same line appears on page 16 of the 1966 edition, and is quoted and critiqued in Allison, *Kant's Transcendental Idealism*, 5. Ameriks comments that Kant's "transcendental idealist ontology implies a kind of immaterialism," but here *immaterialism* refers only to "an insistence on a non-spatio-temporal character for things in themselves." Karl Ameriks, *Interpreting Kant's* Critiques (Oxford: Oxford University Press, 2003), 6. Ameriks suggests that "Kant's famous Refutation of Idealism" rejects the specific form of idealism with which Berkeley is usually identified, namely, the claim "that we know inner matter 'immediately' and can 'only infer' from these to what is outer." Ameriks, *Interpreting Kant's* Critiques, 18.

8. Ameriks, *Interpreting Kant's* Critiques, 1.

9. Cornelius Van Til, *Christianity and Barthianism* (Philadelphia: Presbyterian and Reformed, 1964), 194.

10. Ameriks, *Interpreting Kant's* Critiques, 1.

of material substances, but also followed through with the basic tenet of empiricism more radically than Berkeley, and denied that there are spiritual (mental) substances underlying the subjects of perception—the rational *ego* underlying Descartes's *cogito*. Such spiritual substances, per Hume, are not perceptible to us.

Hume posited that between the Lockean notions of *sensations* and *ideas*, there is something called *impressions*. Impressions are immediately associated with sensation. The feeling of pain associated with a sword cutting into my chest, for example, is an impression. When a sword is only "levelled at my breast," the idea of the painful sensation in my memory or imagination would still be invoked.[11] The term *imagination* does not refer to something fictitious. It is, rather, the idea of a sensation in the absence of actual sensory perception, and this idea comes from past experience. According to Hume, ideas of experience originate from impressions, which constitute the ultimate source of what might in one sense or another be called *knowledge*.

Some ideas, to be sure, are intuitively available to us and do not originate from experience. For instance, "there never was a circle or triangle in nature," but "the truths demonstrated by Euclid" concerning the relations of these ideas "would for ever retain their certainty and evidence."[12] Thus, Hume distinguishes between "matters of fact" and "relations of ideas."[13] The "sciences of geometry, algebra, and arithmetic," as well as "every affirmation which is either intuitively or demonstratively certain," are instances of the latter.[14] These relations are "discoverable by the mere operation of thought."[15]

---

11. David Hume, *An Enquiry concerning Human Understanding and Other Writings*, ed. Stephen Buckle (Cambridge: Cambridge University Press, 2007), 52.

12. Hume, *Enquiry concerning Human Understanding and Other Writings*, 28.

13. Hume, *Enquiry concerning Human Understanding and Other Writings*, 28.

14. Hume, *Enquiry concerning Human Understanding and Other Writings*, 28.

15. Hume, *Enquiry concerning Human Understanding and Other Writings*, 28.

What we consider to be human knowledge, however, comprises for the most part matters of fact, which are "not ascertained in the same manner."[16] Matters of fact are known through experience. But what can we know about such matters? Or do we know what we think we know? Do we, for instance, really know, as a matter of fact, that the sun will rise tomorrow?

Because matters of fact are contingently and not necessarily true, "the contrary of every matter of fact is still possible; because it can never imply a [logical] contradiction."[17] As absurd as it may seem to hold to the belief *"that the sun will not rise tomorrow,"* it is "no less intelligible a proposition, and implies no more contradiction than the affirmation, *that it will rise.*"[18]

"All reasonings concerning matter of fact," Hume contends, "seem to be founded on the relation of *cause* and *effect.*"[19] What we claim to know about "this relation," however, "is not, in any instance, attained by reasonings *a priori*; but arises entirely from experience, when we find that any particular objects are constantly conjoined with each other."[20]

Note here that Hume's usage of the terms *a priori* and *a posteriori* differs explicitly from that of early-modern rationalism. Whereas rationalists such as Wolff define these terms as different modes of demonstration—the former from cause to effect and the latter vice versa—Hume conjoins these notions with experience. In Hume, these two terms refer to two modes of reasoning: *a posteriori* presupposes experience (it is "posterior" to experience), and *a priori* does not (it is "prior" to experience). These definitions will be important for our later discussion of Kant.

16. Hume, *Enquiry concerning Human Understanding and Other Writings*, 28.

17. Hume, *Enquiry concerning Human Understanding and Other Writings*, 28.

18. Hume, *Enquiry concerning Human Understanding and Other Writings*, 29 (italics original).

19. Hume, *Enquiry concerning Human Understanding and Other Writings*, 29 (italics original).

20. Hume, *Enquiry concerning Human Understanding and Other Writings*, 30.

For Hume, causality, unlike the fundamental laws of logic, is not intuitive. The invention of the category of causality arises only after we observe that some objects and events seem to regularly correlate with one another. The fact, however, is that we are only applying inductive reasoning to the objects of experience: we are trying to recognize the correlations between different objects or events when similar patterns are repeatedly observed. Every morning the sun rises, and we conclude from this experience of almost innumerable observations that there is a correlation between morning and sunrise. It is a fallacy, however, to confuse *correlation* with *causation*. Induction only gives us correlations between objects and events, but we can never ascertain any causal relationship between them.

Hume gives the famous billiard-ball example to illustrate this point: we are accustomed to think that a second ball is set in motion as an effect of collision with the first ball. Yet "motion in the second billiard-ball is a quite distinct event from the motion in the first."[21] We inductively gather that every time we see a collision, the second ball is set in motion. Our memory of the correlations between these two events leads us to the "invention" of the category of causality, but the fact is that we have never empirically perceived any cause or effect as an object or event.[22] Reasoning in terms of cause and effect, in other words, is a habit of the mind subjectively developed through experience, and yet not substantiated by experience.

Only *a priori* reasoning provides certainty of thought. All *a posteriori* reasonings are based on the dubitable category of causation. Experience does not guarantee to us that the sun will rise tomorrow, or that every time "a billiard-ball [is] moving in a straight line towards another," the "first ball" will not "leap off

21. Hume, *Enquiry concerning Human Understanding and Other Writings*, 31.
22. Hume, *Enquiry concerning Human Understanding and Other Writings*, 31.

from the second in any line or direction."[23] In fact, on the basis of *a priori* reasoning, all sorts of bizarre events following the motion of the first ball toward the second are theoretically "consistent and conceivable."[24]

Hume would even go so far with the basic tenet of empiricism as to contend that our notions of "material" and "spiritual" (i.e., mental) "substances," just like causality, are merely inventions of our psychological habits.[25] The notion that there are substances behind our ideas of external phenomena arises only from the secret mechanisms of our mental processes that lead to groundless beliefs. When I perceive a white, spherical, slippery, and cold object, for instance, I call it a *snowball*. Hume, as with Berkeley, would contend that there is no such thing as a substance properly called a *snowball*. All that we perceive—all that exist—are the color, shape, and other apparent qualities of what we call a *snowball*. We can never ascertain the existence of a permanent substance behind these appearances.

It is unsurprising that the aforementioned twentieth-century readers of Kant, who adopted basically Berkeleian lines of interpretation, saw no genuine disagreement between Kant and Hume with regard to substance and causality. Once again, this was the intellectual milieu against which Van Til learned to read Kant. On Van Til's account, "Kant said that time and therefore contingency or discontinuity are as ultimate as are the logical principles of continuity. All truth is therefore *de facto*. Rationality is, therefore, nothing in itself. It is what it is for man only as a formal organizing principle of the raw stuff of experience."[26] Van Til takes this to mean that "we have reached an all-time high of nominalistic assertion" in Kant: things "are called beefsteak and pork

23. Hume, *Enquiry concerning Human Understanding and Other Writings*, 32.
24. Hume, *Enquiry concerning Human Understanding and Other Writings*, 32.
25. Hume, *Enquiry concerning Human Understanding and Other Writings*, 64.
26. Van Til, *Christianity and Barthianism*, 204.

chops *by us,* and that is all that matters *for us.* They are what we call them."[27] As we will see, this straw-man interpretation—held by some of the most authoritative Kant scholars of Van Til's time—misses the very point of Kant's textually perspicuous disagreement with Hume. Against Hume, Kant explicitly contends for the permanence of substance and the *a priori* nature of the category of causality (though Kant's notion of *substance* is quite difficult to interpret—it is a principle, rather than something ontological).

Before we turn our attention to Kant, however, we need to explain one more feature of Hume's empiricism, namely, his departure from Berkeley with regard to the existence of the perceiving subject. The "secret mechanism" of psychological habits leading us to believe that there are material substances external to our minds, according to Hume, also gives rise to the belief that there is a permanent spiritual substance that is the subject of one's perceptions and ideas.[28] All that experience gives us, however, are successions of distinct impressions and ideas. The psychological processes of recollection and imagination habitually conjoin impressions and ideas, as well as the present and the past, in such a way that we are led to believe that there is a unified and permanent mental substance that serves as the subject of successive impressions and ideas. There is, however, no *a priori* or *a posteriori* warrant for the supposition of the existence of such mental substances. Put more simply: I cannot be sure whether I really exist as a permanent subject of my experiences. All I have are impressions and ideas that come from experience.

It is hardly surprising, then, that Hume's treatment of causality and substance is usually understood to be characterized by metaphysical skepticism (unlike Descartes's skepticism, which is

27. Cornelius Van Til, *The New Modernism: An Appraisal of the Theology of Barth and Brunner* (Philadelphia: Presbyterian and Reformed, 1946), 25 (italics original).
28. Van Til, *New Modernism,* 64.

only methodological). His attack on traditional understandings of causality is known to have effectively pronounced the unviability of speculative metaphysics, but as Kant sees it, much more is at stake here.

If there were no objectivity to what we think we know about matters of fact in terms of causality and laws of nature, then the accomplishments of the scientific revolution would have been a grand edifice without foundation. Additionally, I would have no way of knowing whether I am indeed interacting with real beings—material or rational—outside myself. Even worse, I would never be sure whether I really am: that is, whether I exist as a permanent substance, a being, whether my *ego* is permanently identical with itself. There are also aesthetic and moral implications to what Kant took to be Hume's subjectivism and skepticism, and Kant found these profoundly troubling as well.

While Kant saw Hume's "concept of cause" as the "*crux metaphysicorum*" threatening all that we reasonably and duly think we know, one problem that concerned him most was the existence of God.[29] Hume's challenges to the knowability of the thinking subject—the *ego cogito*—amounted to a powerful assault on Descartes's ontological argument; his skepticism toward causality placed traditional cosmological and teleological arguments in a precarious position. For Kant, we can make sense of neither the natural nor the moral world if we are deprived of the rational ground for having faith in God's existence. With Hume, Kant rejected traditional metaphysics and, along with it, the kind of rational theology that culminated in Wolff. Kant's intention was nevertheless to ward off what he understood to be Humean skepticism in order to secure what he understood to be the rightful places of science, morality, and religion in modern philosophy and society.

29. Kant, *Prolegomena*, 65.

The Bounds of Human Reason

Synthetic *a Priori* Judgments

One crucial step in Kant's response to Hume is to inquire into the possibility of synthetic *a priori* judgments. In many ways, the question of this possibility is the very question that the first *Critique* seeks to answer. Kant begins with the novel distinction between *analytic* (*analytische*) and *synthetic judgments* (*synthetische Urteile*), a distinction that, in his own words, "no one has previously thought of."[30]

| Simply put, *analytic judgments* are propositions in which the predicate is already included in the subject. The predication "All boys are male," for instance, is analytic. The predicate does not amplify the information given in the subject. Kant calls such predications "judgments of clarification."[31]

| *Synthetic judgments*, by contrast, are "judgments of amplification": they are propositions in which the predicate provides new information not contained in the subject.[32] One such example: "All children are welcome in my house." One cannot analytically deduce from the definition of *children* that I welcome them into my house. In this predication, then, information is amplified by the addition of the predicate to the subject.

As explained earlier, Kant basically adopted Hume's definitions of *a priori* and *a posteriori* judgments: the former is non-empirical ("prior" to experience), while the latter is empirical ("posterior" to experience). Synthetic *a priori* judgments, simply understood, are judgments of amplification in which the subject and predicate involve *a priori* concepts and/or ideas (*concepts* and *ideas* will be defined later).

---

30. Immanuel Kant, *Critique of Pure Reason*, ed. and trans. Paul Guyer and Allen Wood (Cambridge: Cambridge University Press, 2007), B19.

31. Kant, *Critique of Pure Reason*, A7/B10.

32. Kant, *Critique of Pure Reason*, A7/B10.

Synthetic *a posteriori* judgments combine empirical judgments to render new information that is not necessarily true. By contrast, analytic *a priori* judgments are judgments of clarification about nonempirical propositions. They are necessarily true, but do not lead us to knowledge of anything that we did not already know. Only synthetic *a priori* judgments—judgments of amplification that are nonempirical—give us knowledge of new information that is necessarily true. Human knowledge and science, in other words, hinges on the very possibility of synthetic *a priori* judgments.

That synthetic *a priori* judgments are possible is, according to Kant, clearly indicated by the science of arithmetic. He gives the famous example of "7 + 5 = 12."[33] One might be misled to think that this is merely an analytic judgment about the number "12" as a conceptual composite of "7" and "5." But, claims Kant, the definition of "7" is not contained within the definition of "5," while "+" and "=" are notions of which the definitions are not contained in numbers. Because every sign in this equation represents an *a priori* concept, the equation amounts to a synthetic *a priori* judgment.

According to Kant, Hume had only a very vague conception of the synthetic-analytic distinction. Kant commends Hume for having come "closest" among "all philosophers" to the notion of synthetic *a priori* judgments.[34] Hume, as Kant sees it, rightly points out that the development of human knowledge requires synthetic judgments. Hume, however, unwittingly restricted synthetic judgments to *a posteriori* reasoning, and associated them with the allegedly dubitable "connection of the effect with its cause."[35]

Kant concurs that "judgments of experience . . . are all

33. Kant, *Critique of Pure Reason*, B13–18.
34. Kant, *Critique of Pure Reason*, B19.
35. Kant, *Critique of Pure Reason*, B19.

synthetic."[36] But he points out that Hume committed a fallacy by concluding from this that all synthetic judgments are *a posteriori*. As a result, even Hume overlooked "the real problem of pure reason," namely: "How are synthetic judgments *a priori* possible?"[37]

In other words, Hume thought that all synthetic judgments were *a posteriori* and could never be necessarily true. According to Kant, Hume was right about traditional metaphysics: it consisted of analytic *a priori* and synthetic *a posteriori* judgments, which were nothing but predications of clarification rendering no new information, combined with propositions of amplification providing no necessary truth. Kant contends, however, that metaphysics de facto done this way does not mean that metaphysical knowledge is impossible.

It is worth our while here to expand on the *a priori–a posteriori* distinction that Kant inherited from Hume and combined with the analytic-synthetic distinction. Recall that in traditional philosophy up to Wolff, *a priori* and *a posteriori* designated two modes of argumentation: the former denotes demonstration from cause to effect, and the latter vice versa. Hume redefined these two notions in terms of experience.

Kant, as we just saw, basically adopts Hume's definitions. But Kant makes some subtle yet important clarifications. *A posteriori* cognition is "that which is *merely* borrowed from experience," that is, that which is "cognized . . . only empirically."[38] Kant agrees with Hume that judgments merely borrowed from experience give us "no true universality" and do not bear the "character of inner necessity."[39] Yet Kant thinks that Hume failed to see that

36. Kant, *Critique of Pure Reason*, A7/B11.
37. Kant, *Critique of Pure Reason*, B19.
38. Kant, *Critique of Pure Reason*, A2 (italics added). Note here that Kant's disagreement with Hume is already obvious in the first edition of the *Critique*, even though his engagement with Hume in this edition is not as explicit as the second, or his *Prolegomena*.
39. Kant, *Critique of Pure Reason*, A1.

this does not lead to the conclusion that our experiences never involve or depend on anything that is universal and necessary— things that do not depend on experience and on which experience depends. Hume's mistake, in other words, stemmed from a subtle yet elementary *non sequitur* fallacy.

Following Hume, Kant defines *a priori* cognition as the kind of cognition whose justification is independent of experience. Kant ascribes to *a priori* cognition three basic criteria: (1) universality, (2) necessity, and (3) purity. Universality is conjoined with necessity, and they are defined in terms of independence from experience: "universal cognitions, which at the same time have the character of inner necessity, must be clear and certain for themselves, independently of experience; hence one calls them *a priori* cognitions."[40]

This criterion of independence from experience is the basic meaning of *purity*. The word *pure* (*rein*) can have a variety of meanings in Kant's writings. Sometimes it is synonymous with *a priori*, but if *a priori* only implies the conditions of universality and necessity, then purity encompasses these conditions. There are also different degrees and types of purity. For example, a "pure" cognition is one "that is not mixed with anything foreign to it," but "a cognition is called absolutely pure . . . in which no experience or sensation at all is mixed in, that is thus fully *a priori*."[41]

Many readers approaching Kant for the first time have the impression of a juxtaposition between *pure* and *practical* reasons in his vocabulary. This confusion understandably arises from the titles of the first two *Critiques*—that of "pure reason" and that of "practical reason." The reader should bear in mind, however, that *practical* reason can also be *pure*—it can cognize universal and

---

40. Kant, *Critique of Pure Reason*, A1.
41. Kant, *Critique of Pure Reason*, A10–11.

necessary truths entirely *a priori*. Kant's dichotomy is between theoretical and practical reason, instead of the pure and the practical. He gives to *pure reason* (*reine Vernunft*) the basic definition "that which contains the principles [*Prinzipien*] for cognizing something absolutely *a priori*."[42] (A *principle* is a logical and/or ontological starting point with which we can explain given truths and realities.)

In his explanation of the purity of *a priori* cognition, Kant makes a fundamentally anti-Humean move. He contends that "if one removes from our experiences everything that belongs to the senses, there still remain certain original concepts and the judgments generated from them, which must have arisen entirely *a priori*, independently of experience."[43] The reason is that such *pure concepts* (defined below), derived entirely *a priori*, are the very things that "make one able to say more about the objects that appear to the senses than mere experience would teach, or at least make one believe that one can say this, and make assertions contain true universality and strict necessity."[44] This is something "the likes of which merely empirical cognition can never afford."[45]

Kant's argument here is intended to demonstrate an anti-Humean point that is "especially remarkable": "even among our experiences cognitions are mixed in that must have their origin *a priori* and that perhaps serve only to establish connections among our representations of the senses."[46] In other words, Kant is arguing against Hume that synthetic judgments involving experience must depend on pure concepts that arise entirely *a priori*, or else there can be no empirical knowledge at all.

42. Kant, *Critique of Pure Reason*, A11/B24.
43. Kant, *Critique of Pure Reason*, A2.
44. Kant, *Critique of Pure Reason*, A2.
45. Kant, *Critique of Pure Reason*, A2.
46. Kant, *Critique of Pure Reason*, A2.

Kant's "Copernican" Shift: Modest Objectivity

Note that Kant does not ask *whether* objective knowledge is possible. The "real problem of pure reason," as we saw earlier, is *how* such knowledge is possible, which is to ask: "How are synthetic *a priori* judgments possible?"[47] Kant makes it textually clear in the introduction to the first *Critique*, especially in the second edition, that he takes the objectivity of human knowledge for granted. Ameriks calls this the "commonsense starting point of Kant's arguments," namely, "that there is some objectivity to our experience, that some of our states (of a basic kind, i.e., perceptual, moral, aesthetic) are not mere private events but can be justified and are true or false."[48]

Ameriks calls this a *regressive approach*: Kant starts with what has been objectively given to our cognitive faculties and works his way back to sorting out how our empirical knowledge has been made possible. On this reading, Kant's approach to knowledge is diametrically opposed to both Cartesian and Humean skepticism, in that he rejects the egocentric coordinate systems of Descartes and Hume.

That Ameriks's interpretation of Kant is correct in this respect is, as far as I can see, shown by what is plainly set forth in Kant's text from the outset of the first *Critique*. In asking how knowledge (synthetic *a priori* judgments) is possible, Kant names three specific fields of knowledge: pure mathematics, natural science, and metaphysics.[49]

Arithmetic is, for Kant, the most obvious case of a science that consists of synthetic *a priori* judgments (recall his famous example of $7 + 5 = 12$). Geometry and Newtonian physics were also widely regarded in Kant's time as being comprised in true knowledge, and he saw no reason to cast any doubt on their

47. Kant, *Critique of Pure Reason*, B19.
48. Ameriks, *Interpreting Kant's* Critiques, 89.
49. Kant, *Critique of Pure Reason*, B20.

scientific status. It did not require meticulous work on his part to show that they also consist of synthetic *a priori* judgments. Thus Kant: "About these sciences, since they are *actually given*, it can appropriately be asked *how* they are possible; for that they *must be* possible is *proved* through their actuality."[50]

The question, now, is whether metaphysical knowledge is also something that Kant takes for granted as the starting point of his regressive reasoning. The simple answer from the plain meaning of the text is yes. This question, however, has been complicated since Kant's own day by misrepresentations of his first *Critique* as an antimetaphysical treatise. The truth is, he was opposed only to the kind of dogmatic approach to metaphysics that Wolff exemplified.

Kant is very clear on this point: "unavoidable contradictions have always been found in *all previous attempts* to answer" the great questions of metaphysics, such that "one can and must regard as undone all attempts made *until now* to bring about a metaphysics dogmatically."[51] On his view, the problem with traditional metaphysics is that previous philosophers generally started with analytic *a priori* judgments and imposed these speculative propositions of clarification on synthetic *a posteriori* judgments. The gap between necessary truths of reason and contingent matters of fact can never be bridged this way.[52]

That metaphysics had not de facto enjoyed the same success as mathematics and physics, however, was no reason for Kant to cast it out from philosophy. Like pure mathematics and natural science, metaphysical knowledge was an actuality that he took for granted as the starting point of his regressive critique of pure reason.

Kant makes it clear that metaphysical knowledge consists in a "kind of cognition" that "is in a certain sense also to be regarded

50. Kant, *Critique of Pure* Reason, B20 (italics added).
51. Kant, *Critique of Pure Reason*, B22–23 (italics added).
52. Kant, *Critique of Pure Reason*, B23.

as given."[53] Indeed, "metaphysics is *actual*, if not as a science yet as a natural predisposition . . . ; a certain sort of metaphysics has *actually* been present in all human beings . . . , and it will also always remain there."[54] Thus, the question must be addressed: "How is metaphysics as a natural predisposition possible?"[55]

Kant takes for granted that this natural predisposition gives rise to rightful claims of some form of knowledge, even though the traditional discipline of metaphysics had been adulterated with ungrounded claims "moved by the mere vanity of knowing it all."[56] Early-modern rationalists thought that human reason was capable of establishing a God's-eye view of things and even of God. It was this egocentric presumption of theocentric knowledge characterizing Descartes's methodological skepticism that inescapably led to Hume's metaphysical skepticism.

Kant's critique of reason is not intended to be antimetaphysical, but rather antiskeptical. He acknowledges that we do possess natural knowledge of metaphysical things, and so the "last question" that "flows from the general problem" of pure reason (i.e., the possibility of synthetic *a priori* judgments) "would rightly be this: How is metaphysics possible as a science?"[57]

Kant recognizes metaphysics as "a science that is indispensable for human reason."[58] Speaking specifically of metaphysics, he states that "the critique of reason thus finally leads necessarily to science."[59] He likens metaphysics to a plant deeply rooted in the nature of human reason that no one will ever be "able to eradicate."[60] His critique of reason is intended to give rise to a new

53. Kant, *Critique of Pure Reason*, B21 (italics added).
54. Kant, *Critique of Pure Reason*, B21 (italics added).
55. Kant, *Critique of Pure Reason*, B21.
56. Kant, *Critique of Pure Reason*, B21.
57. Kant, *Critique of Pure Reason*, B22.
58. Kant, *Critique of Pure Reason*, B24.
59. Kant, *Critique of Pure Reason*, B22.
60. Kant, *Critique of Pure Reason*, B22.

"approach" to metaphysics "entirely opposed to the previous one, in order to promote the productive and fruitful growth" of this science by chopping down "every stem that has shot up" from human hubris.[61]

Kant's critique of reason, then, attempts to establish what we can and cannot know, in such a way that our knowledge claims will always seek to remain *modest* (a term that scholars have used to describe his project). The immodest, uncritical, and unlimited use of human reason "without critique," characteristic of traditional metaphysics, leads to "groundless assertions, to which one can oppose equally plausible ones, thus to skepticism."[62]

The modest character of Kant's program is textually perspicuous: he proposes that "self-denial" is "required" in order to "give up all these claims" to metaphysical knowledge that are in fact no more than illusions.[63] This modesty, I should contend, lies at the very heart of Kant's "Copernican" shift in the theory of knowledge. His claim is that absolutely objective knowledge pertains to God alone, and that philosophy's pretentious attempt at such knowledge is destructive to objectivity.

Since Kant's own day, many have interpreted his "Copernican" shift as an epistemological "turn to the subject," placing the human subject of knowing at the center of a coordinate system. Students of Van Til's apologetics are especially prone to think that Kant makes man the measure of all things. All truth claims become subjective in the Kantian system. This popular misreading directly contradicts Kant's thesis.

So what, exactly does Kant mean when he employs the Copernican analogy? Most interpreters today agree on what is set in the immediate context. In the preface to the second edition of the first *Critique*, he compares his revolution in metaphysics

61. Kant, *Critique of Pure Reason*, B22.
62. Kant, *Critique of Pure Reason*, B22.
63. Kant, *Critique of Pure Reason*, B24.

to the contribution of "Copernicus, who, when he did not make good progress in the explanation of the celestial motions if he assumed that the entire celestial host revolves around the observer, tried to see if he might not have greater success if he made the observer revolve and left the stars at rest."[64] Kant proposes that "in metaphysics we can try in a similar way regarding the intuition of objects" (the term *intuition* will be explained below).[65] If we assume with the early-modern rationalists and empiricists that our empirical ideas are entirely adventitious (from without), then we cannot avoid Berkeleian subjectivism and Humean skepticism, for then there would be nothing *a priori* in our empirical knowledge. As Kant puts it, if empirical cognition "has to conform to the constitution of the objects, then I do not see how we can know anything of them *a priori*."[66]

Only God perceives things as they are in themselves. To say that our perception can conform to the constitution of the objects is to say that we can know things as they are in themselves. Allison helpfully points out that this kind of absolute objectivism characterizing rationalist metaphysics amounts to a "theocentric model, with its ideal of an eternalistic, God's-eye view of things."[67]

Kant's "Copernican" shift seeks to establish an anthropic way of knowing, in which we perceive things as they appear to us, and as our cognitive faculties present them to ourselves. In other words, if we hypothesize that "the object (as an object of the senses) conforms to the constitution of our faculty of intuition," then we can very well proceed to discuss the "possibility" of establishing synthetic *a priori* knowledge of the object.[68]

64. Kant, *Critique of Pure Reason*, Bxvi.
65. Kant, *Critique of Pure Reason*, Bxvi.
66. Kant, *Critique of Pure Reason*, Bxvii.
67. Allison, *Kant's Transcendental Idealism*, 28–29.
68. Kant, *Critique of Pure Reason*, Bxvii.

The proposal here is that our knowledge of things can enjoy modest (but never absolute) certainty and objectivity only if we recognize that our cognition actively interacts with external objects, for "we can cognize of things *a priori* only what we ourselves have put into them."[69] The reason is that *a priori* conditions pertain to our concepts, and not to the objects that we perceive. The recognition of the relative (not essential or fundamental) subjectivity of our cognition is the key to establishing (essentially and fundamentally) certain and objective knowledge qua human knowledge.

This new approach, of course, will have to meet a number of challenges, of which Kant is well aware. The central "difficulty" is that if our cognition can be at all objective, then we must assume not only that the constitution of external objects conforms to our perception, but that our perception conforms to these objects as well.[70] Yet does the latter assumption not lead us right back to the same difficulty of traditional metaphysics?

Here Kant resorts to the faculty of the *understanding*. External objects do not immediately conform to our sensible cognition. Rather, they conform to our intellectual understanding. We do not just perceive objects with our senses and leave our sensory data in a disorganized state. We use our intellectual faculty to think and understand these objects. Kant takes for granted that we already possess objective understanding of things. This means that there must be some rational order in the external world analogous to the intellectual and rational structure of our minds, in such a way that each of us can interact with other material and spiritual beings.

In other words, the fact that we can think the world means that the world must be capable of being thought. Kant does not

69. Kant, *Critique of Pure Reason*, Bxvii.
70. Kant, *Critique of Pure Reason*, Bxvii.

see any need to justify this basic assumption: we have to start from here; otherwise, we cannot make sense of the fact that we do make sense of many matters of fact. In his own words, "the attempt to think them [objects of experience] . . . will provide a splendid touchstone of what we assume as the altered method of our way of thinking"—"for they *must be* capable of being thought."[71]

Discursivity: Sensibility and Understanding

This two-way traffic between thinking and that which is thought is sometimes called Kant's *discursivity thesis*.[72] To say that human cognition is *discursive* (*diskursiv*) is to say that it necessarily involves an interplay between two cognitive faculties that are distinct from each other, namely, *sensibility* and *understanding* (defined below). These two cognitive faculties give rise to different types of what Kant calls *representations*.

Anglophone readers approaching Kant's text for the first time can be thrown off by the frequent occurrence of this peculiar term, which seems to vary widely in meaning from one passage to another. In fact, Kantian vocabularies in general can be quite confusing. In the rest of this section, I will present a basic framework of some of his key terms. Because the information below is largely uncontroversial, I will limit my use of citations in order to avoid distracting readers coming into Kant's terminological labyrinth for the first time.

Let us begin with the aforementioned term, *representations* (*Vorstellungen*). Literally, the verb *vorstellen* means "to put forth."

71. Kant, *Critique of Pure Reason*, Bxvii (italics added).
72. Allison's exposition of this thesis has set a standard in Kant studies, though it has been subjected to debate in the literature for decades. Ameriks has suggested that Allison's depiction of Kant's idealism can in fact be reconciled with that of one of his chief opponents, Paul Guyer. See Allison, *Kant's Transcendental Idealism*; Karl Ameriks, "Kantian Idealism Today," in *Interpreting Kant's* Critiques, 98–111.

Vorstellung, in its everyday usage, can carry a number of designations, including "conception," "notion," "perception," "belief," "view," "presentation," and "introduction." The standard English translation of this Kantian term comes from the philosopher's own use of *Vorstellung* as the German equivalent of the Latin *repræsentatio*. In traditional philosophy, *repræsentatio* refers generically to all the ways in which something is presented to the mind. All cognitive acts of the mind are thus called *representations*. So, for example, the formation of an empirical concept in the mind can be called a *representation*. For Kant, conceptual representations can be *a priori* or *a posteriori*. A concept itself can also be called a *representation*.

Kant's usage of the term breaks with the rationalist tradition in a significant way. From Descartes to Wolff, *repræsentatio* is by definition intellectual. Descartes, for example, says that sensory objects are represented to us not by the senses, but rather by the faculty of thinking. In the famous "wax argument," he contends that our senses give to us only the shape, color, texture, smell, and other sensible characteristics of a piece of wax, but that when it is heated, these characteristics change. The fact that we still represent it as wax after the change means that above and beyond its sensible characteristics there must be an intelligible substance that we call *wax*. This ontological substance that is intelligible is represented to us not by the senses, but rather by the intellect.

Taking seriously Hume's critique of rationalism without buying into Humean skepticism, Kant insists that although we must presuppose permanent substance[73] as a principle (as opposed

---

73. The "principle of permanent substance" is the first of Kant's three "Analogies of Experience." Discussion of the three Analogies would involve some very advanced debates in Kant studies, not least because Kant's own presentation of the matter is fraught with gaps, if not inconsistencies (as some have alleged), in his argumentation. His textual treatments of the first Analogy in the two editions of the first *Critique* differ significantly also. Scholars generally agree that Kant is not speaking of an ontological substance. Rather, he is referring to something permanent relative to changes

to something ontological) underlying the objects represented to our minds in space and time, our intellect is incapable of immediately grasping ontological substances. Objects can be represented to the mind only indirectly by our own cognitive faculties. Each external object is individually given to our minds through sensible experience, and our faculty of the understanding then gathers and processes these raw materials to give rise to cognition.

Cognition (*Erkenntnis*) is a family of representations that features prominently in the first *Critique*. I like to define it in simple terms as the process by which we make sense of sensible things. This process is perceptive and objective. It is perceptive in that it is a conscious representation, and objective in that it is directed toward the object. Cognition gives rise to judgments (explained earlier), which are the smallest units of knowledge.

In order to make sense of sensible things, two preconditions must be fulfilled: (1) some sensible thing of which to make sense must be given to our minds, and (2) our minds must possess something *a priori*, with which to make sense of the sensible things given. Note that sometimes Kant uses *cognition* in a looser sense, such that a sensible *intuition* (defined below) can also be called a *cognition*.

Fulfilling the first precondition above is the task of *sensibility* (*Sinnlichkeit*). This is the cognitive faculty that represents to our minds the objects that appear to our senses. The representation of an object that we receive through sensibility is not *the thing in itself* (*das Ding an sich*), the ontological substance of the object, which the ancient Greeks and early-modern rationalists thought to be intelligible (like the substance of wax in Descartes's argument). The term *noumenon* (*Noumenon*) is often, but not always, used interchangeably with *the thing in itself*. A noumenon stands

---

in time, so that when we intuit an object in time, we have this permanent substance as our point of reference. In other words, permanence is a precondition for temporal relations. See Kant, *Critique of Pure Reason*, A183/B226.

in juxtaposition to a *phenomenon* (*Phänomen*). The latter is an object of sensibility; the former is the ontological substance of an object above and behind its phenomena. Sensibility represents to us the object *as it appears* to our senses. What is given to the mind through sensibility, then, is not the ontological substance of the object, but rather its *appearance* (*Erscheinung*).

There is a difference between appearances and phenomena. Appearances are representations that precede our conceptual use of the understanding, while representations of the objects of experiences that ensue from the intellectual comparison of appearances are called *phenomena*. While appearance is contrasted to the thing in itself, the noumena-phenomena distinction is a closely related but somewhat distinct binary. In any case, sensibility as described above is an overall (though not completely) passive faculty: it makes a representation only when it is acted on by an external object that appears to us, for our cognitive faculties are incapable of originating appearances.

When our capacity to represent is acted on by the appearances of external objects, a representation called *intuition* (*Anschauung*) arises as an immediate response mechanism of the cognitive faculty of sensibility. The German word *Anschauung* literally means "to look at" or "to gaze upon," and this literal meaning says a lot about what it expresses metaphorically. The act of looking at something is directed toward the object that is being looked at. As far as experience is concerned, an intuition is the immediate representation of an individual object to the mind. This representation is an act of the faculty of sensibility directed toward the object. The object appears to our senses, and we intuit it through sensation.

Empirical intuition as such is to be distinguished from *sensation* (*Empfindung*), in that sensations are directed toward the mind, rather than the object. More precisely, a sensation consists in the *effect* (*Wirkung*) of an object on our cognitive capacity for representations. Sensation as such is what makes sensibility an overall passive faculty, despite its act of intuition. That is, empirical intuition arises only as a response mechanism to sensation.

Not all intuitions are empirical, however. Kant distinguishes between two kinds of sensible intuitions that human beings can possess, namely, pure and empirical intuitions. *Pure intuitions* (*reine Anschauungen*) are entirely unmixed with experience, and serve as the *a priori* precondition for empirical intuitions. More precisely, they are the representations of space and time as the very form of our sensible intuitions. *Empirical intuitions* (*empirische Anschauungen*), explained above, relate to objects through sensations within the representations of space and time. In this way, even sensibility—not just the intellect—involves something pure and *a priori*.

Before proceeding, I realize that many Anglophone readers have found the term *intuition* confusing, because Kant's definition clearly does not accord with our everyday usage of the word. What he has in mind is obviously not some "sixth sense" or mysterious instinct. Yet it is important to retain this standard English translation, because Kant uses the German word *Anschauung* as a rendering of the Latin philosophical term *intuitus*.

The most basic definition of *intuitus* is "immediate cognition" or "immediate representation." But what can we cognize immediately? Here, Kant takes issue with his predecessors again. Descartes is well representative of rationalist philosophy when he asserts that his famous *cogito* ("I think") is an intuition, something that we cognize immediately. That is, we do not need to reflectively deduce the "I think": it is intuitively true and certain. From this intuition, we can draw the conclusion, *ergo sum* ("therefore I am").

Now, if we apply Kant's criterion of synthetic *a priori* judgments to Descartes's argument from intuition, we can see that "I think, therefore I am" is in fact an "analytic proposition," if the

"I am" is taken to signify the existence of the thinking subject.[74] It would be a predication of clarification that leads to nowhere, because "I think" already presupposes "I am."

If, with the Cartesian tradition, the "I am" is taken to signify a simple substance, however, then the problem is much more severe. The concept of *simple substance* is not included within "I think," and to conclude from the "I think" the reality of such a simple substance amounts to a leap of faith in a "synthetic proposition," "as if" the conclusion were given "by a revelation."[75] Kant calls Descartes's "miraculous" faith in the *ego* the "poorest representation of all."[76] For Kant, our intellect is incapable of intuiting anything, not even the spiritual substance of our thinking self.

While Kant insists that all human intuitions are sensible, he also acknowledges that the kind of *intellectual intuitions* (*intellektuelle Anschauungen*) with which rationalist metaphysics sought to view the self, the world, and God can, in theory, exist as well. He juxtaposes intellectual intuitions to *sensible intuitions* (*sinnliche Anschauungen*). The latter requires the existence of an object that produces an effect on our capacity to represent: we cannot intuitively represent an object *ex nihilo*. The former, by contrast, represents an object entirely out of nothing, and does not depend on the existence of the object or its effect on the capacity to represent. In this sense, sensible intuitions are said to be *derivative*, while intellectual intuitions are said to be *original*.

Kant is emphatic that "our kind of intuition" qua human intuition can only be sensible.[77] We cannot intellectually intuit objects without sensibility, which presupposes sensation. That is, we cannot represent objects immediately with the intellect alone.

74. Kant, *Critique of Pure Reason*, B407.
75. Kant, *Critique of Pure Reason*, B407.
76. Kant, *Critique of Pure Reason*, B407.
77. Kant, *Critique of Pure Reason*, B307.

The only intellect that does not require sensibility in intuiting objects is that of God.

To say that God's intuition is intellectual is the same as saying that his intellect is intuitive, and his understanding immediate.[78] There is no need for deduction or reflection in God's mind, nor does he need to experience matters of fact in order to know them, for he possesses immediate knowledge of all things. That is, God knows all things all at once, and his cognition is unconfined by space or time.

Human beings, however, are not omniscient. Our intuition can only be sensible. We intuit objects only through space and time, and we can intuit them only after they produce an effect on our cognitive capacity to represent. Our intuition as such can never be intellectual, and this also means that our intellectual cognition (i.e., understanding) can never be intuitive: we cannot cognize things as God.

Human cognition requires the application of the concepts of the understanding to our sensible intuitions. In other words, human cognition must be discursive; it can never be intuitive. The discursivity thesis, in this light, serves to underscore the limitations of human cognition as the cognition of creatures and not God: "the cognition of every, at least human, understanding is a cognition through concepts, not intuitive but discursive."[79]

The term *understanding* (*Verstand*) here refers to another primary faculty of cognition. It is an active faculty, in that it applies rational concepts to objects that are given to our minds by sensibility, so that we can make sense of sensible things. Kant uses this term as a German rendering of the Latin *intellectio*. Whereas rationalism generally holds that we cognize with our intellect and not our senses, Kant insists that this cognitive faculty on its own

78. Kant, *Critique of Pure Reason*, B70–72.
79. Kant, *Critique of Pure Reason*, A68/B93.

would be empty and futile. As the faculty that thinks, understanding needs sensibility to provide that which is thought by it. Conversely, without understanding, sensibility would be fruitless, for all its representations would be blind and meaningless. As Kant famously puts it, "Thoughts without content are empty, intuitions without concepts are blind."[80]

The primary representation of the understanding is called *concept* (*Begriff*). Concepts are contrasted to intuitions in two important respects. First, although concepts and intuitions are both objective (i.e., they address objects), intuitions are singular and particular, while concepts refer to a plurality of objects in their universality. Think of a cat, for example. My intuition does not give me the concept of a cat. What I intuit is something furry that has an extension in space and moves in time (in fact, even *furry* is a conceptual interpretation of what I intuit). The cat that I happen to intuit may be small and black in one particular instance, and large and white in another. Sensibility alone cannot tell me that in both instances the object of my cognition is a cat. It is my understanding that gathers and processes individual intuitions to produce the empirical concept of a cat.

Second, we can see from the illustration above that intuitions are immediate, while concepts operate in indirect and complex manners. We use concepts of various sorts to synthetically represent new concepts. For instance, when we understand cats to be animals that are adept in catching rats, we are synthesizing different concepts that we previously represented from experience. We also understand that the existence of each cat has a cause in time.

In the foregoing illustration, we can gather two types of concepts: empirical and pure. One that is represented from experience is called an *empirical concept* (*empirischer Begriff*), which is

---

80. Kant, *Critique of Pure Reason*, A51/B76.

a posteriori. There is, of course, quite a gap between individual intuitions and their *synthesis* (*Synthese*) into an empirical concept. The word *synthesis* here refers generally to the mental act of gathering and conjoining different representations, in order to represent them in one cognition. In the synthesis of manifold intuitions into a concept, the act is spontaneous.

The cognitive faculty responsible for syntheses in general is the *power of imagination* (*Einbildungskraft*). This function of the mind is for the most part subconscious, and Kant admits that we know precious little about how it works. We do know that it is there, however, because the synthesis of intuitions in the production of empirical concepts would not have been possible otherwise.

In addition to empirical concepts, Kant stresses that we must possess concepts that do not depend on experience. These include concepts such as *existence* and *causality*, which we possess before representing any actual cat, or anything else actually existent or caused. Such a concept is represented entirely *a priori*, and as such it is called a *pure concept* (*reiner Begriff*). The pure concepts of understanding are crucial for enabling synthetic judgments to be *a priori*.

Kant explicitly follows Aristotle in calling the pure concepts *categories* (*Kategorien*), but moves beyond Aristotle in grounding the formulation of the categories on the principle of *judgment* (*Urteil*). The categories are intended to be an exhaustive account of the logical functions of the understanding, which we apply to objects given to the mind to form judgments. All the categories are there in our minds, and unlike the case of the imagination, we are conscious of how our minds operate with the categories. Unlike empirical concepts, which are innumerable because we never stop imaginatively synthesizing new concepts from contingent experiences, the categories are numerically exhaustible because they are in our minds, and the conscious functions of our minds are limited. Below is Kant's famous "table of categories."[81]

1.
Of Quantity

Unity
Pluraliy
Totality

2.		**3.**
Of Quality		**Of Relation**
Reality		Of Inheritence and Subsistence
Negation		(*substantia et accidens*)
Limitation		Of Casualty and Dependence
		(cause and effect)
		Of Community (reciprocity
		between agent and patient)

4.
Of Modality

Possibility—Impossibility
Existence—Nonexistence
Necessity—Contingency

To say that the categories are *a priori* is to say that they are built-in functions natural to the construct of the human intellect. Take the category of causality as an example. It is within our nature to look for causes. Imagine, for instance, that your cell phone somehow will not turn on, but you know that the battery is well and alive. As you exclude the possibility of a dead battery, you start to look for other causes of the malfunction. When you realize that you cannot find the cause on your own, you take your device to a repair shop. You will be disappointed if the expert tells you that he, too, fails to find the cause, but you will not think that he is lying. On the other hand, if he tells you that the cell phone is simply dead without a cause, you will find his excuse outrageous. Naturally, we assume that everything has a cause, and innumerable experiences of not being able to

---

81. Kant, *Critique of Pure Reason*, A80/B106.

find the causes of certain things do not lead us to abandon this assumption. The category of causality, then, is pure. That is, it is a concept independent of experience, and experience can neither validate nor invalidate it.

Because the categories are pure and *a priori*, they serve to provide pure syntheses of representations, which give rise not only to the unity of representations in an intuition, but also to the unity of representations in a judgment. The combination of empirical and pure concepts, in other words, makes synthetic *a priori* judgments in the field of experience possible. I can judge, for example, that motion in the second billiard ball is somehow caused by collision with a first ball, even if my theoretical explanation of the precise nature of the cause may be flawed. Such judgments constitute the smallest units of *knowledge* (*Wissen*).

Now, if the understanding is the cognitive faculty that combines concepts to form judgments, then *reason* (*Vernunft*) is the higher faculty responsible for synthesizing judgments to form coherent systems of knowledge. A coherent system of knowledge consisting of synthetic *a priori* judgments on a particular family of objects is called a *science* (*Wissenschaft*). As Kant sees it, Hume's failure to recognize the *a priori* character of the category of causality blinded him to the possibility of synthetic *a priori* judgments, and Humean skepticism is ultimately destructive to the sciences.

Note that Kant does not feel the need to deduce the *a priori* nature of a category such as causality, or to prove that theoretical use of the categories is legitimate. Such pure concepts spring forth from the very nature of human reason, and it makes no sense for us to doubt them. If we do not trust the categories with which our understanding is endowed, we cannot explain the fact that we do possess empirical knowledge and sciences. Kant, again, is not interested in the skeptical question whether we know what we think we know. Assuming that objects are given to us to be known, and that humankind has possessed some form of scientific knowledge (however primitive it may be) ever since our ancestors were created, he wants to find out how objective knowledge and science have been made possible.

It is also worth pointing out here that in our foregoing analysis, Kant is emphatic that conceptual cognition of objective reality is possible only within a drastically limited domain of representational capabilities, and this differentiates him not only from his rationalist and empiricist predecessors, but also from German idealists of the ensuing generation. His use of the term *concept* (*Begriff*) is indicative of this point.

The German noun *Begriff* is from the verb *greifen*, which literally means to "grab" or "grasp." Idealists such as Hegel developed the originally Kantian terms *concept* and *representation* (*Vorstellung*) in a speculative direction that sought to revive the Cartesian tradition in a distinctively post-Kantian way. In Hegel, representational understandings are associated with sensibility, while conceptual understanding is to grasp the rational essence of something.

Hegel, after Kant, acknowledges that conceptual understanding cannot be immediate. It can be attained only through reflective interpretation of historical phenomena. Whereas idealists of Hegel's generation variously proposed that the human race can consummately develop some quasi-divine conception of reality that is absolute, however, Kant is consistently at pains to emphasize that human and divine cognitions can never be identical in any sense. For Kant, our intellectual concepts can never grasp the ontological essence of objective reality.

Furthermore, whereas Hegel posits a consummate identity between our concepts and the logical structure of reality, Kant denies that there is any ontological link or analogy between our categories and the objects known by us. According to Kant, there is only a formal analogy between the rational structure of the human mind and that of the world of objects. Our *a priori* concepts, then, can help us to make sense only of the appearances of objects that are represented to the mind, which presupposes the existence of empirical objects from which our *a posteriori* concepts originate. Only God has conceptual access to things in themselves, and all his concepts are entirely pure and *a priori*: he does not need to experience things in order to know them. This is because God's conception of objects does not presuppose their existence. Rather, his conception of these objects gives rise to their existence. God alone, then, possesses *a priori* concepts of objects outside his being. Kant's "Copernican" revolution in philosophy, in this respect, is intended to remind us: eating from the tree of knowledge is destructive to human knowledge, for we can never know as God.

Transcendental Idealism

Underlying Kant's theory of knowledge, presented above, is his famous and difficult doctrine of transcendental idealism. Interpretational problems associated with this doctrine have been central to debates in Anglophone Kant studies in recent decades. The good news is that leading scholars in the field today generally make clearly discernible the various emphases that they place on text, context, and contemporary reader responses. This means that we will be able to choose an interpretive model that honors both text and context in the most comprehensive manner.

Now, I realize that the term *transcendental idealism* can sound very intimidating, and its implications can be even more confusing than the terminology. The good news is that there is a basic definition to which all scholars would agree, and this definition is not nearly as esoteric as the terminology might make it seem.

Simply put, *transcendental idealism* (*tranzendentaler Idealismus*) is the doctrine that human beings can experience only the appearances of external objects, but not things in themselves.

More precisely, human intuition can only represent appearances, while ontological constitutions of the things that we intuit are not identical with their appearances to us. Concomitantly, the doctrine states that space and time are not real objects external to our cognitive faculties, but rather the very forms of the human intuition that makes our experience of appearances possible.

Now, we might wonder what this definition has to do with the words *transcendental* and *idealism*. Here the term *transcendental* is to be distinguished from *transcendent*. *Transcendent* is juxtaposed to *immanent*. Noetically (i.e., from the subjective perspective of the knower), *transcendent* qualifies principles beyond the boundaries of possible experience, while *immanent* describes principles that lie within these boundaries. Ontically (referring to the object itself), the transcendent "pertains to nature so far as its cognition can be applied in experience (*in concreto*)," and the immanent "to that connection of the objects of experience which surpasses all experience."[82] The ontic aspect of the transcendent-immanent distinction has sometimes been neglected in the literature, but the text here clearly shows that this distinction is not merely concerned with the theory of knowledge. Some things transcend our knowledge because they transcend nature. This distinction thus carries a manifestly metaphysical dimension.

But again, *transcendental* (*tranzendental*) is not to be confused with *transcendent*. *Transcendent* qualifies objects of cognition; *transcendental* qualifies cognitions. The transcendent is beyond the reach of experience and thus unknowable, while the transcendental is independent of experience (i.e., *a priori*). All transcendental cognitions are *a priori*, but not all *a priori* cognitions are transcendental. In both editions of the first *Critique*, Kant gives a definition of *transcendental* early on in the introduction, when he "call[s] all cognition transcendental that is occupied not so much

---

82. Kant, *Critique of Pure Reason*, A846/B874.

with objects but rather with our mode of cognition of objects insofar as this is to be possible *a priori*."[83] In this way, the adjective *transcendental* can modify a wide range of nouns. For example, Kant dedicates considerable length to the "transcendental deduction" of the aforementioned "categories."

I like to think of *transcendental* in simpler terms as a form of cognition that ascends above cognition itself, to cognize *that* and *how* we cognize entirely *a priori* in some of our representations. As Kant himself explains, *transcendental* refers to the ways in which "we cognize *that* and *how* certain representations (intuitions or concepts) are applied entirely *a priori*, or are possible."[84] This definition shows that he takes the possibility of *a priori* intuitions and concepts—and, as it follows, synthetic *a priori* judgments—for granted. He does not ask *whether* they are possible. Rather, having transcendentally cognized *that* they are possible, he wants to find out *how*.

The *whether* is to be asked not with regard to the possibility of empirical knowledge, but with regard to the ideality or reality of the very forms of our cognition. To be precise, Kant has in mind the sensible forms of our intuition, namely, space and time. He is decidedly a transcendental idealist, which means that he subscribes to *idealism* (*Idealismus*) as far as the transcendental forms of our intuition are concerned. An idealist is "someone who ... does not admit that it [the existence of external objects] is cognized through immediate perception and infers from this that we can never be *fully* certain of their reality from any possible experience."[85]

A transcendental idealist, then, holds that all appearances "are all together to be regarded as mere representations and not as things in themselves, and accordingly that space and time are

---

83. Kant, *Critique of Pure Reason*, A11/B25.
84. Kant, *Critique of Pure Reason*, A56/B80 (italics added).
85. Kant, *Critique of Pure Reason*, A368 (italics added).

only sensible forms of our intuition, but not determinations given for themselves or conditions of objects as things in themselves."[86]

The term *determination* (*Bestimmen*) here is an important notion recurring throughout Kant's writings. He defines it in a way that builds on Wolff's use of the term. We saw earlier that Wolff envisions reality in terms of his philosophy of possibles. The reality of life on earth, for instance, is a factual possible; it is also possible, though counterfactual, that there is no life on earth. That there is life on earth not only is possible and factual, but also becomes determinate, when we give a reason not only why there is life on earth, but also why the contradictory possible is excluded. Kant takes this definition further by proposing the notion of a *complete determination*: something is completely determinate when the sum total of all its possible predicates is considered in relation to the contradictory opposite of each predicate. I am human, and not nonhuman; I was born in Taiwan, and not elsewhere; I am a subject of Her Majesty the Queen of Canada, and not the Mikado of Japan. My determination as Alex Tseng is the ground of all that I am and all that I am not. Kant retains the rationalist view that reality is ultimately rational and not contingent. This means that there must be ultimate reasons why some possibles are factual and why some are not.

Space and time are not determinations of things in themselves that can remain when they are abstracted from the subjective conditions of human cognition. Kant thus speaks of the *transcendental ideality* (*tranzendentale Idealität*) of space and time, which means that they become "nothing as soon as we leave out the condition of the possibility of all experience, and take [them] as something that [grounds] the things in themselves."[87]

86. Kant, *Critique of Pure Reason*, A369.
87. Kant, *Critique of Pure Reason*, A28/B44.

This is not to say that space and time are not real or objective in our everyday understanding of the words *objectivity* and *reality*. Kant emphasizes that the transcendental ideality of space and time goes hand in hand with their *empirical reality* (*empirische Realität*), that is, "objective validity," in our everyday understanding of the words.[88] There are doubtless objective ways to measure extensions in space and durations in time to which we can all agree. Kant himself was impeccably punctual, and it has often been said that the people of Königsberg would adjust their watches in accordance with his daily walking routine through the city. What he means by the transcendental ideality and subjectivity of time and space is that they are the *a priori* preconditions of our intuition of all objects, and as such they are unlike any object.

Kant notices that we intuit objects in and through space and time, but we do not really intuit space and time as objects. One side of a table, for instance, is of a certain length in space, but we do not intuit an object that we eventually conceptualize as length. Rather, we intuit an object that has an extension in space, which we in turn conceptualize as a table. Similarly, we do not intuit time itself. We intuit a spherical object off the left hand of Arnoldis Chapman. We do not intuit the duration of its motion from his hand to Gary Sánchez's glove. Rather, duration is the form by which we intuit the object in motion, which we then conceptualize as a four-seam fastball. This shows that we do not intuit time. We, with time as a sensible form of reference, intuit objects that are in time. In this sense, space and time are the "transcendental forms" of our sensibility, and they are transcendentally ideal (again, *ideal* simply means that something pertains to the mind, rather than to objective reality outside the mind).

Furthermore, this ideality entails that space and time are entirely *a priori* and pure (unadulterated with experience). Let

88. Kant, *Critique of Pure Reason*, A27/B44.

us demonstrate this by considering the case of the ideality of space. The thrust of Kant's argument is that our sensations do not take up any space as a table or a chair does. Yet our sensations of the table and the chair are represented in spatial relations. This means that our representation of space precedes our capability to sensibly represent the table and the chair in space. Because the representation of space precedes any experience of spatial objects, it must be *a priori*.

Kant opposes this transcendental idealism—especially the transcendental ideality of space and time—to *transcendental realism (tranzendentaler Realismus)*.[89] Transcendental realism "regards space and time as something given in themselves (independent of our sensibility). The transcendental realist therefore interprets outer appearances (if their reality is conceded) as things in themselves, which would exist independently of us and of our understanding."[90]

Kant's claim here is that if space and time are regarded as real objects of empirical intuition, like a table or a four-seam fastball, then what we intuit would be things in themselves, rather than

89. This is the point at which interpretation of Kant becomes controversial. The meaning and express intent of his text are in fact quite clear, and the debate is mainly whether Kant can consistently uphold his claims that space and time are transcendentally ideal, but empirically real. Can he avoid the implication that the appearances of empirical objects are completely subjective? The pivotal point in the debate is whether the thing in itself and its appearance are two different objects, or two aspects of the same object. Furthermore, if they are two aspects of the same object, are they so distinct from each other that we can practically treat them as two objects? All would agree that things in themselves are real. The point of contention is whether appearances are also real in the sense that they are somehow analogous to things in themselves. While Kant's text is certainly open to different exegetical options, I see no reason to read into his text a framework that he clearly rejects. While the two-object theory has fallen out of favor in contemporary Kant studies, scholars such as Paul Guyer and Rae Langton still tend to treat the two-aspect theory in a way that sometimes borders on two-object interpretations. See Recommended Reading for information on contemporary debates surrounding Kant's transcendental idealism.

90. Kant, *Critique of Pure Reason*, A21.

their appearances. The reason, implicit in the quote above but spelled out at length in the *Critique*, is basically that the transcendental ideality of space and time ascribes to our sensible intuitions an unavoidable degree of subjectivity, such that we intuit the appearances of things only in, with, and through space and time. If we could empirically intuit space and time, then the veil of appearances would be lifted, and things in themselves would be intelligible to us.

This realist view of the utter objectivity of sensible intuitions, according to Kant, does not lead to objectivity in empirical knowledge. As shown in the previous section, he thinks that when we take the forms of our own sensible intuitions to be objective and absolute points of reference, such an attempt at a God's-eye view of things ultimately leads to the destruction of objectivity.

Thus Kant: "It is really this transcendental realist who afterwards plays the empirical idealist."[91] Allison explains that "Kant is here arguing that transcendental realism leads to *empirical idealism* [*empirischer Idealismus*], which is the doctrine that the mind can have immediate access only to its own ideas or representations, that is, the familiar Cartesian-Lockean theory of ideas."[92] The gist of Kant's argument can be reformulated as follows: (1) Transcendental realism holds to the major premise that the objects of our sensible intuition are things in themselves, rather than their appearances. (2) Transcendental realism holds to the minor premise, along basically Cartesian-Lockean lines, that we have intuitive access only to our own ideas. (3) Therefore,

91. Kant, *Critique of Pure Reason*, A369.
92. Allison, *Kant's Transcendental Idealism*, 21 (italics added). Allison's appeal to this passage in support of his interpretation carries the burden to prove that Kant's position stated here in the first edition of the *Critique* is retained in the second. That this is indeed the case is suggested by passages that Allison quotes from the second edition, but he does not make it explicit. This is an instance of my point that his meticulous reading of the text could have been enriched and nuanced by greater emphases on the context.

transcendental realism cannot avoid the conclusion that the supposed things in themselves that we intuit are nothing other than ideas in our minds. We can never be sure whether the objects of our sensible representations really exist outside our minds.

Kant's *transcendental idealism* is expressly intended to safeguard *empirical realism* (*empirischer Realismus*), the doctrine that our subjective experience somehow corresponds to objective reality by means of complex analogies. As he puts it plainly, "the *transcendental idealist* is an *empirical realist*, and grants to matter, as appearance, a reality which *need not be inferred*, but is immediately perceived."[93]

His transcendental idealism, then, is not an empirical idealism, which he explicitly rejects, but rather a *formal idealism* (*formaler Idealismus*). Ameriks explains that this "position ... denies only the absolute reality of these formal [i.e., spatiotemporal] determinations and not the existence of things themselves."[94] For Kant, transcendental acknowledgment of the limits and subjectivity of our cognition is the only way to explain the fact that we do possess objective knowledge of the world; it is the only way to defuse the dangers of the obviously absurd skepticism of Berkeleian-Humean empirical idealism that the Cartesian-Lockean view of ideas ultimately leads to.

Some scholars have duly noted that Kant's transcendental idealism, along with the empirical realism and formal idealism that it entails, serves to underscore his consistent intent to contend that human cognition can never attain to any God's-eye view of things.[95] God is not within the confines of space and time, and he does not intuit things in those forms. As explained earlier, God intuits all things intellectually. All our intuitions and cognitions are finite and sequential, but God knows all things in

93. Kant, *Critique of Pure Reason*, A371 (italics added).
94. Ameriks, *Interpreting Kant's* Critiques, 21.
95. Including, notably, Allison and Ameriks, as cited earlier.

infinite representations and utter simultaneity. God's knowledge as such is entirely and exhaustively objective. Our knowledge, on the other hand, is bound to the finitude and sequentiality of spatiotemporality, and thus an unavoidable degree of subjectivity. "We can accordingly speak of space [and time]," and spatiotemporal objects, "only from the human standpoint. If we depart from the subjective condition[s] under which alone we can acquire outer intuition, namely that through which we may be affected by objects, then the representation[s] of space [and time] signif[y] nothing at all."[96] Humble recognition of the transcendental subjectivity of human cognition—the recognition that we are not God—is required, if we have any hope of safeguarding the empirical objectivity of our knowledge and cognition. Kant's emphasis on the subjectivity of human knowledge and cognition, then, is diametrically opposed to subjectivism, solipsism, relativism, and skepticism.

Faith and Hope: Kant on Morality and Religion

Overview: Kant's Major Works on God and Morality

Kant is, on his own account, an empirical realist and transcendental idealist in the theoretical use of reason. There is, however, yet another dimension to his philosophy, according to one of the most traditional interpretations of his works. In the practical use of reason, he should be understood as a transcendental realist. That is, he makes rational existence claims of the ideas of God, freedom, and immortality. This reading can be traced back to Kant's contemporary Karl Leonhard Reinhold (1757–1825), and has been affirmed by Kant himself, despite dissatisfactions and reservations on Kant's part.[97] Although

96. Kant, *Critique of Pure Reason*, A26/B42.
97. See Karl Reinhold, *Letters on the Kantian Philosophy*, ed. Karl Ameriks, trans. James Hebbeier (Cambridge: Cambridge University Press, 2005).

secularist and naturalist interpretations dominated much of Kant scholarship in the twentieth century, there has been a resurgence of this religious and theological reading since the 1990s.[98]

On this interpretation, which I take to be evidently true to Kant's texts and context, his philosophical discourse on the idea of God is negatively limited only by the epistemological and metaphysical boundaries set in the first *Critique*. Positively, it takes a moral approach to theology and religion, in order for reason to extend itself to God as an object of knowledge that it cannot reach within theoretical bounds.

This may initially seem to call into question Kant's denial of the scientific status of theology. His frequent references to theology as a science may lead the reader to wonder whether there is a fundamental contradiction in his view. In the first *Critique*, as we saw, he explicitly states that metaphysics and theology can be scientific. Even in his later works, he would speak of "biblical theology" (theology developed on the basis of biblical revelation) as a "science."[99] But the fact remains: from the second *Critique* (*Critique of Practical Reason*) onward, he explicitly dismisses the scientific status of any form of theology. Even a proponent of the "religious Kant" such as Professor Stephen Palmquist would remind us that Kant effectively denies "all scientific *knowledge* of God."[100] Whenever Kant refers to theology as a science, then, he should be understood as using the word in a very loose sense. He regards theology as a matter of faith bordering on practical knowledge (*what ought to be*)—which is, to be sure, grounded in reason—rather than theoretical knowledge (*what is*).

98. An important landmark in this interpretational trajectory is Chris L. Firestone and Stephen R. Palmquist, eds., *Kant and the New Philosophy of Religion* (Bloomington: University of Indiana Press, 2006).

99. E.g., Immanuel Kant, *Religion within the Bounds of Bare Reason*, trans. Werner S. Pluhar (Indianapolis: Hackett, 2009), 7.

100. Stephen R. Palmquist, "Introduction," in Kant, *Religion*, xix (italics original).

The first edition of the first *Critique* already forecasts Kant's moral approach to theology. His first systematic attempt at moral metaphysics is the 1785 *Groundwork to the Metaphysics of Morals* (*Grundlegung zur Metaphysik der Sitten*). Dissatisfied by the inconsistencies and ambiguities of this work, he composed the famous 1788 *Critique of Practical Reason* (*Kritik der praktischen Vernunft*), published a year after the second edition of the first *Critique*. Still, some central claims of this work were to be revised in later writings.

While the 1797 *Metaphysics of Morals* (*Metaphysik der Sitten*) is generally acknowledged as the most mature formulation of Kant's moral philosophy, *Religion within the Bounds of Bare Reason* (*Religion innerhalb der Grenzen der blossen Vernunft*), published in 1793 and 1794, is a milestone in which Kant corrects the problematic theses set forth in his previous works.[101] Because our purpose is to offer a theological assessment of Kant's thought in the next chapter, I will focus on the development of his theology that culminates in *Religion*. We will have to start with the first *Critique* in order to know what he means by the "bounds of bare reason." We begin here with an introduction to the notion of *transcendental theology*, a pivotal point of transition from theoretical to practical reason in Kant's first two *Critiques*.

God, in Theory: Transcendental Theology

Kant's appeal to practical reason is a significant move in his philosophy. Theoretical reason is concerned with *what is*, practical reason with *what ought to be*. In the *Critique of Practical Reason*, he sets forth the thesis that the ideas of freedom, immortality,

---

101. For instance, despite his otherwise problematic interpretation, Paul Guyer rightly points out that "by the time of his *Religion within the Boundaries of Mere Reason* . . . , Kant clearly does withdraw the thesis of the *Groundwork*, that the mere existence of freedom of the will is a sufficient condition for autonomy." Paul Guyer, *Kant's System of Nature and Freedom* (Oxford: Oxford University Press, 2005), 124.

and God, which are transcendent and regulative in the theoretical use of reason, become "immanent and constitutive" within the "practical capacity" of "pure reason."[102]

The term *regulative principle* (*regulatives Prinzip*) refers to a logical and ontological starting point (this is the basic definition of a *principle*) that, among other possible starting points, directs the understanding to the highest degree of unity and coherence, but the validity of which we can never know for sure—not even by a *reductio ad absurdum*. A regulative principle "can be presupposed only as optional and contingent."[103] A *constitutive principle* (*konstitutives Prinzip*), by contrast, is a *postulate* (*Postulat*) that we can ascertain by reason, so long as this postulate provides a "certain determinate condition" that is "absolutely necessary" for what we know to be true and real.[104]

Kant's claim in the second *Critique* is that in our *practical reason*, the ideas of God, freedom, and immortality become immanent and constitutive to us. The practical use of reason provides a ground for the extension of theoretical reason to objects that are otherwise transcendent and unascertainable. That is, we can form synthetic *a priori* judgments about them as real objects: these "objects . . . have now been given to it [theoretical reason] on practical grounds and . . . only for practical use."[105]

To appreciate the importance of this claim, we need to start with Kant's treatment of transcendent ideas and transcendental theology in the first *Critique*. He distinguishes between *idea* (*Idee*) and *concept*. Ideas are a special species of pure concepts. Causality and existence, as seen earlier, are examples of pure concepts of the understanding. Ideas, on the other hand, are pure

102. Immanuel Kant, *Critique of Practical Reason*, ed. and trans. Mary Gregor (Cambridge: Cambridge University Press, 1997), 141.

103. Kant, *Critique of Pure Reason*, A632/B660.

104. Kant, *Critique of Pure Reason*, A632/B660.

105. Kant, *Critique of Practical Reason*, 141.

concepts of reason, the cognitive faculty responsible for synthesizing judgments to form coherent systems of knowledge.

Kant uses *idea* in dialogue with traditional metaphysics, particularly the rationalist notion of *innate ideas*. In the first *Critique*, he offers lengthy discussions of the ideas of the soul, the world, and God, in response to the Wolffian divisions of rational psychology, rational cosmology, and rational theology. His basic claim is that traditional metaphysical treatments of these ideas fall short of synthetic *a priori* judgments, and in their analytic speculation, no determination about any of these ideas can be made (see definition of *determination* above). Rational cosmology, for instance, unavoidably falls into *antinomies*, a situation in which every predication of the idea (e.g., the existence of the world is caused) and its contradictory opposite (e.g., the world is uncaused and self-existent) can be proved by equally valid arguments or counterarguments.

The belief that we have determinate knowledge of the objects to which these transcendent ideas supposedly refer, according to Kant, is an *illusion* (*Illusion*; *Schein*). We innately possess ideas such as God, and the illusion that we cognize real objects to which these ideas refer arises from the very constitution of our intellectual and rational faculties. Kant compares the unavoidability of this kind of illusion to the way that, to our eyes, "the sea appears higher at the middle than at the shores."[106] Transcendental critique of our cognition reveals the core beliefs of rational metaphysics to be mere illusions.

The illusions of rational theology are discussed under the rubric of "the ideal of pure reason." An *ideal* (*Ideal*) is the individual concretion of an idea, "that is, as an individual thing, determinable or even determined by the idea alone."[107] Kant gives

---

106. Kant, *Critique of Pure Reason*, A297/B353–A298/B354.
107. Kant, *Critique of Pure Reason*, A568/B596.

simpler definitions of the terms in the third *Critique* (*Critique of the Power of Judgment*): "**Idea** signifies, strictly speaking, a concept of reason, and **ideal** the representation of an individual being as adequate to an idea."[108] God is, strictly speaking, the only true ideal, though Kant also speaks of ideals such as that "of the beautiful," which he identifies as the concretion of the "archetype of taste."[109]

In the first *Critique*, Kant argues in the chapter on the ideal of pure reason that all rational attempts to prove God's existence are "entirely fruitless," for "the principles of reason's natural use do not lead at all to any theology."[110] As the ideal of pure reason, the idea of God is a regulative principle without which there can be no systematic unity in our knowledge. That is, without the idea of God as the very ideal of pure reason—as the concretion of the universal idea of supreme and original being—our knowledge would be left in bits and pieces. But God is not a constitutive principle in the theoretical use of reason apart from practical reason, and all theoretical-rational proofs of God's existence are nothing but *dialectical* (by which Kant basically means "sophistic" and "contradictory") illusions.

Among these is "the illusion of [the] logical necessity" of God's existence in the ontological argument of rationalist metaphysics.[111] Kant's refutation of Descartes's ontological proof is lengthy, but the crux of it is simple: *existence* is not an attribute, so it does not analytically pertain to the concept of a perfect being in the same way as, say, *omnipotence* does. God is, by conceptual definition, perfect; perfection, by definition, includes

---

108. Immanuel Kant, *Critique of the Power of Judgment*, ed. Paul Guyer, trans. Paul Guyer and Eric Matthews (Cambridge: Cambridge University Press, 2000), 117 (boldface original).

109. Kant, *Critique of the Power of Judgment*, 117.

110. Kant, *Critique of Pure Reason*, A636/B664.

111. Kant, *Critique of Pure Reason*, A594/B622.

omnipotence. Thus, the concept of an almighty deity without the attribute of omnipotence would indeed be logically self-contradictory. But a proposition that negates the existence of the very subject of predications such as "God is omnipotent" also negates all its predicates, so there would be no logical contradiction in such a proposition. Kant explains this with the analogy of a triangle: "To posit a triangle and cancel its three angles is contradictory; but to cancel the triangle together with its three angles is not a contradiction."[112]

Put another way, because God is the ideal of pure reason in whom no attribute is contingent, propositions describing God's attributes, such as "God is omnipotent," are all analytical. Such propositions are true by conceptual necessity, but they say nothing of God's existence. All existential predications, by contrast, are synthetic: "God exists" is a proposition that synthesizes two distinct concepts—*God* and *existence*. No synthetic proposition can be true by logical necessity: "this privilege pertains only in the analytic propositions, as resting on its very character."[113]

Analytic propositions about the idea of God, however, cannot be the determination of a real being, for determination necessarily involves synthetic judgments. In the theoretical use of reason, the idea of God becomes determinate to us only when it is measured against another object, but because God is the original and highest being, there is no being against which God's being can be measured. If God is indeed the only true ideal of pure reason—an idea of the highest rank—then it can never satisfy the criterion of determinacy (being affirmed or negated on the ground of an other). Descartes thought that he could affirm God's existence by the authority of the *cogito* alone, but the Cartesian project became disillusioned after Kant. The

---

112. Kant, *Critique of Pure Reason*, A594/B622.
113. Kant, *Critique of Pure Reason*, A589/B626.

cogito—sheer speculative thinking—is incapable of determining the synthetic proposition "God exists." The very "illusion" of the Cartesian proof consists precisely "in the confusion of a logical predicate with a real one (i.e., the determination of a thing)."[114]

In the concluding section of the chapter on God as the ideal of pure reason, Kant distinguishes between different kinds of theology. He defines *theology* in broadest terms as "cognition of the original being" that we call *God*.[115] Rational theology (*theologia rationalis*) is cognition of God "from pure reason," revealed theology (*theologia revelata*) "from revelation."[116]

In both editions of the first *Critique*, Kant says nothing about revealed theology beyond mere definition. Some have argued that this silence had to do with political censorship that forbade philosophers to publish in writing any criticism of Christian theology, but this censorship started only in late 1786 and would not have applied to the first edition. We need to recognize that this silence is entirely consistent with his critique of rational theology. His express intention is to critique human reason, not faith; and his intention in the critique of human reason, as he explicitly states in the preface to the second edition, is "to deny knowledge in order to make room for faith."[117] He might well have tailored to political expectations, but we must not forget how he identifies the assumption of the limitless powers of human reason in the "dogmatism of metaphysics" as the "true source of all unbelief conflicting with morality."[118] There is, aside from political motives, this important philosophical reason why Kant is not interested in pursuing revealed theology in his critique. His focus is on rational theology.

114. Kant, *Critique of Pure Reason*, A589/B626.
115. Kant, *Critique of Pure Reason*, A631/B659.
116. Kant, *Critique of Pure Reason*, A631/B659.
117. Kant, *Critique of Pure Reason*, Bxxx.
118. Kant, *Critique of Pure Reason*, Bxxx.

Rational theology can be of two kinds. *Transcendental theology* (*tranzendentale Theologie*) "thinks its object . . . merely through pure reason, by means of sheer transcendental concepts."[119] Here the term *transcendental* is continuous with the definitions given earlier, with the additional implication and connotation that what is transcendental can be neither proved nor disproved by experience. By contrast, *natural theology* (*natürliche Theologie*) thinks its object "through a concept which it borrows from nature (the nature of our soul) as the highest intelligence."[120] Whereas transcendental theology appeals to pure reason alone, natural theology resorts to experience. Natural theology as such, per Kant, cannot be truly theological on its own, for apart from transcendental concepts, it ultimately reduces God to nature. "If the empirically valid law of causality is to lead to an original being, then this would have to belong to the causal chain in objects of experience; but then it, like all appearances, would have to be conditioned."[121] What natural theology on its own renders, then, is "far from any concept of a highest being, because for us experience never offers us the greatest of all possible effects."[122]

The question of God's existence is transcendental, and "transcendental questions admit only of transcendental answers . . . , without the least of empirical admixture."[123] The difficulty is that this question "is obviously synthetic and demands an extension of our cognition beyond all the boundaries of experience, namely to the existence of a being that is supposed to correspond to our mere idea, to which no experience can ever be equal."[124] This is precisely why Descartes's ontological proof, a prime example of

119. Kant, *Critique of Pure Reason*, A631/B659.
120. Kant, *Critique of Pure Reason*, A631/B659.
121. Kant, *Critique of Pure Reason*, A636/B664.
122. Kant, *Critique of Pure Reason*, A637/B665.
123. Kant, *Critique of Pure Reason*, A637/B665.
124. Kant, *Critique of Pure Reason*, A637/B665.

transcendental theology, can never provide a determinate answer to the transcendental question of God's existence.

It is important to recognize, however, that Kant in fact ascribes to transcendental theology a high degree of eminence. He takes for granted our cognition of God as a real object and transcendental clarifications of the idea of God as necessary in both the theoretical and practical uses of reason. Although transcendental theology on its own gives us only illusions about the idea of God and not true cognition of God, it "retains an important negative use."[125] Its "very great utility" consists in "correcting the [*given*] cognition of this being [God] by making it agree with itself and with every intelligible aim, and by purifying it of everything that might be incompatible with the concept of an original being, and of all admixture of empirical limitations."[126]

Furthermore, even though transcendental theology cannot determine the existence of God, it is at least able to "determine this concept on the transcendental side . . . as the concept of a necessary and most real being," which "would be of the greatest importance."[127] It can at least "get out of the way all opposed assertions, whether they be atheistic, deistic, or anthropomorphic"—"all this is very easy to do in such a critical treatment."[128] What Kant means is that although rational theology in general cannot positively prove or disprove the existence of God, transcendental theology is easily capable of demonstrating the analytic inconsistencies of nontheistic positions. This is important for the theoretical use of reason because, as we saw earlier, without presupposing God's existence as a regulative principle, there can never be any unity or coherence in our systems of knowledge.

125. Kant, *Critique of Pure Reason*, A640/B668.
126. Kant, *Critique of Pure Reason*, A640/B668.
127. Kant, *Critique of Pure Reason*, A640/B668.
128. Kant, *Critique of Pure Reason*, A640/B668.

Faith and Moral Duty

One of Kant's most famous statements in the first *Critique* is that his entire philosophical "interest" is "united" in three questions: "1. What can I know? 2. What should I do? 3. What may I hope?"[129] The three *Critiques* are supposed to correspond to these three questions in order. The *Critique of Pure Reason* is primarily concerned with the first question; the *Critique of Practical Reason* the second; and the *Critique of Judgment*, supposedly, the third. The first question is primarily theoretical; the second, practical; and the third, a bridge between the two.

Kant defines *theoretical cognition* (*theoretische Erkenntnis*) and *practical cognition* (*praktische Erkenntnis*) in simple terms: the former is "that through which I cognize **what exists**," and the latter "that through which I represent **what ought to exist**."[130] Accordingly, the "theoretical use [*Gebrauch*] of reason is that through which I cognize a priori (as necessary) that something is; but the practical use is that through which it is cognized a priori what ought to happen."[131]

The transition from theoretical reason to practical reason is explicitly forecast in both editions of the first *Critique*. As explained earlier, God is, per Kant, only a regulative principle in the theoretical use of reason. We can never prove or disprove the theoretical claim "God exists." Yet God becomes a constitutive principle in the practical use of reason: we can judge with certainty, "God ought to exist."

One central claim of the second *Critique* is stated in the first: "there are practical laws that are absolutely necessary (moral laws)," and the existence of God "has to be postulated" in order to explicate them.[132] Yet in the second *Critique*, Kant shows only

---

129. Kant, *Critique of Pure Reason*, A804/B832–A805/B833.
130. Kant, *Critique of Pure Reason*, A632/B660 (boldface original).
131. Kant, *Critique of Pure Reason*, A632/B660.
132. Kant, *Critique of Pure Reason*, A632/B660.

how our moral agency presupposes the reality of the metaphysical idea of freedom, while the precise roles of the other two ideas— God and immortality—in pure practical reason are not at all clear.

The second *Critique* is in many ways a reworking of *Groundwork of the Metaphysics of Morals* (1785). There, Kant sets forth the all-important notion of a *categorical imperative*, the crucial juncture at which human nature, freedom, autonomy, and the supreme moral law converge. Interpretation of this notion is almost as highly disputed as transcendental idealism, and here we have to settle with a very basic definition.

An *imperative* (*Imperativ*) is a proposition expressing a possible free action that realizes a certain end. Whereas theoretical reason is concerned with indicatives (*what is*), practical reason is preoccupied with imperatives (*what ought to be*). Kant distinguishes between two kinds of imperatives: *hypothetical* and *categorical*. A hypothetical imperative is not universally or absolutely valid. Its moral-rational validity is contingent on the end that it is aimed at achieving, and so it is not an end in itself. For instance, hard work is not an end in itself. It is good only if one works hard for a good end.

The *categorical imperative* (*kategorischer Imperativ*), by contrast, is not directed toward the achievement of an end, but rather it is an end in itself. It is, as such, defined by three formulae: (1) the formula of universality (the law of nature); (2) the formula of humanity; and (3) the formula of autonomy. The first of these is central to the definition of the categorical imperative. It is, in fact, the very imperative itself: "there is . . . only a single categorical imperative, and it is this: *act only according to that maxim through which you can at the same time will that it become a universal law*."[133]

133. Immanuel Kant, *Groundwork of the Metaphysics of Morals*, ed. and trans. Mary Gregor and Christine Korsgaard (Cambridge: Cambridge University Press, 2012), 33 (italics original).

Here, the term *maxim* (*Maxime*) can be understood as a subjective principle of the will, which a person subjectively determines by her or his own reason as the standard for moral actions. For example, one can adopt the maxim that suicide is permissible on the principle of self-love, when the protraction of life brings about more suffering than enjoyment.[134] The question is whether this maxim of self-love can become a universal law. Kant takes for granted the unity and coherence of *the* universal law, and the test for whether a maxim can become a universal law is to examine whether it accords with other universal moral laws of nature. The moral law dictates that we have a perfect duty to promote and protect human life, and so a maxim that allows for the destruction of life cannot possibly become a universal law. By inference, all other maxims based on the principle of self-love, such as the supposed moral lawfulness of borrowing money for the sake of personal need without the intention of returning it, are excluded by the categorical imperative.

The foregoing examples point toward the second formula of the categorical imperative, which states: "act that you use humanity, in your own person as well as in the person of any other, always at the same time as an end, never merely as a means."[135] In the case of suicide or euthanasia, one would be making use of one's own person not as an end in itself, but "merely as a means, to preserving a bearable condition up to the end of life."[136]

This notion of humanity—and all rational beings—as an end and not merely a means toward an end lies at the core of the celebrated Kantian notion of human *dignity* (*Würde*). We are members of the *kingdom of ends* (*Reich der Zwecke*), in which everything has either a price or an "inner worth" called *dignity*.[137]

134. Kant, *Groundwork*, 34.
135. Kant, *Groundwork*, 41.
136. Kant, *Groundwork*, 41.
137. Kant, *Groundwork*, 46.

Something that has a price is exchangeable with some other thing of equal worth. Dignity, on the other hand, is that inner worth "elevated above any price, and hence allows of no equivalent," for it is an end in itself, and not a means toward another end.[138] The success of the commercial slogan "There are some things money can't buy" reflects just how deeply embedded this understanding of dignity is in our culture: it has not enjoyed the same kind of success in my own ancestral country, where it is (still) generally supposed that everything has a price.

There are, of course, things within the realm of human existence that money can buy. Stephen Curry and Jeremy Lin are worth different prices in the NBA. "Skill and diligence in work have a market price; wit, lively imagination, and humor have a fancy price."[139] Things pertaining to our moral nature, such as "fidelity in promising and benevolence from principles (not from instinct)," however, have an "inner worth" that is priceless.[140] Human beings have dignity precisely because we are rational beings endowed with moral reason.

This leads to the third formula of the categorical imperative, namely, "the idea *of the will of every rational being as a universally legislating will*."[141] This is the very idea of *autonomy* (*Autonomie*): "*Autonomy* is . . . the ground of the dignity of a human and of every rational nature."[142]

Kant's notion of *autonomy* is often misunderstood as a state of independence from God. There is some truth to this secularist reading of Kantian autonomy. The word is composed of the Greek *auto* ("self") and *nomos* ("law"), and Kant means thereby *self-legislation*. In his earlier works in the Critical period, there are

---

138. Kant, *Groundwork*, 46.
139. Kant, *Groundwork*, 46.
140. Kant, *Groundwork*, 46.
141. Kant, *Groundwork*, 43 (italics original).
142. Kant, *Groundwork*, 47 (italics original).

strong suggestions that *autonomy* means human self-legislation apart from God's revelation. Kant's mature understanding of God as supreme moral legislator outside the human being is not clearly spelled out in these works—sometimes it is even denied. In the *Groundwork*, for instance, human autonomy means that "every rational being, as an end in itself, must be able to view itself as at the same time universally legislating with regard to any law whatsoever to which it may be subject, because it is just this fittingness of its maxims for universal legislation that marks it out as an end in itself."[143]

Autonomy and dignity are closely related to Kant's notion of human *freedom* (*Freiheit*). There are many apparent inconsistencies in both the *Groundwork* and the second *Critique*. In the third *Critique*, he offers a more coherent account of these notions, but it is not until *Religion* that he offers a mature formulation of freedom in relation to dignity. The basic definitions given in the *Groundwork*, however, are retained throughout his career, and these constitute his moral-metaphysical answer to a transcendental problem raised in the first *Critique*.

In the first *Critique*, Kant considers the dialectic between *determinism* and indeterministic *freedom*. According to the former, "everything . . . happens solely in accordance with the laws of nature," and there is no genuine freedom of the will.[144] The latter, by contrast, insists on a "lawless faculty of freedom" that precludes any adequate notion of "nature."[145] According to Kant, both views are transcendentally invalid, and the metaphysical idea of freedom remains an illusion within theoretical reason.

When we transition from the *is* to the *ought to*, however, this problem is purportedly resolved. Genuine, positive freedom, per Kant, is autonomy, which is knowing and doing what we ought

143. Kant, *Groundwork*, 49.
144. Kant, *Critique of Pure Reason*, A445/B473.
145. Kant, *Critique of Pure Reason*, A449/B477.

to do: to abide by the universal law of our moral nature in every *choice* (*Willkür*) of the *will* (*Wille*). A will governed by *animal instinct* (*arbitrium brutus*) is not free. Only a will to carry out the categorical imperative given to our moral nature is genuinely free. The freedom of autonomy, then, presupposes *negative freedom*, which is noncoercion of the will. If the moral law were imposed on us, we would be under *heteronomy* (under the rule of another legislator), and thus not autonomous.

Now, one reason why Kant's discourse on autonomy and dignity is often understood as a secularist one may be that in the *Groundwork*, where he first presented these notions, God is seldom mentioned. In the second *Critique*, he brings God into the picture as one of the three metaphysical ideas that become constitutive and immanent in the practical use of reason, along with freedom and immortality. Among these three, however, freedom is the only idea of which "the possibility we know *a priori*," for it is the only one on which the reality of the moral law, "which we do know," hinges.[146] This reality does not depend on God as the supreme Lawgiver. In fact, Kant still speaks of human moral agents as the "lawgiving members of a kingdom of morals."[147] He even considers attribution of supreme lawgiving agency to the "will of God" a position of "heteronomy," an assertion that he would later qualify in the third *Critique*.[148]

A view stated in the second *Critique* that Kant retains until the end of his career is that God, as a constitutive principle of which we can make an existence claim, is not an object of knowledge, but an object of faith. In the second *Critique*, Kant contends that God's existence is to be postulated, but not as supreme Lawgiver. Rather, the will of an intelligent God as the highest good is to be postulated as "the supreme determining ground

146. Kant, *Critique of Practical Reason*, 4.
147. Kant, *Critique of Practical Reason*, 68.
148. Kant, *Critique of Practical Reason*, 54.

of the [human] will," which pertains to the faculty of desire in which we make choices, in accordance either with brute instinct or with reason and understanding.[149] The possibility of a "highest derived good" that has yet to be actualized in this world must presuppose "the reality of a highest original good, namely the existence of God."[150]

The reason why this presupposition does not qualify as knowledge is that within the strictly theoretical use of reason, it is only a hypothesis that is beyond rational proof. In the practical use of reason, however, the presupposition of God's existence becomes a matter of rational *faith* (*Glaube*). Kant defines *faith* "as *habitus*, not as *actus*": it is "reason's moral way of thinking in the affirmation of that which is inaccessible for theoretical cognition."[151] Because its object is beyond theoretical cognition, faith does not qualify as knowledge. Faith is rational, however, insofar as it makes a postulation that is necessary for making sense of the realities or possibilities that are known to us. In this sense, faith differs from "opinion": the latter is characterized by mere "credulity," and is entirely groundless.[152] The constitutive postulation of God's existence "in relation to the intelligibility of an object given us by the moral law (the highest good), and consequently of a need for practical purposes, . . . can be called belief [*Glaube*] and, indeed, a pure rational belief since pure reason alone (in its theoretical as well as in its practical use) is the source from which it springs."[153]

Kant goes so far as to claim that "the doctrine of Christianity . . . gives on this point a concept of the highest good (of the kingdom of God) which alone satisfies the strictest demand of

149. Kant, *Critique of Practical Reason*, 101.
150. Kant, *Critique of Practical Reason*, 101.
151. Kant, *Critique of the Power of Judgment*, 335.
152. Kant, *Critique of the Power of Judgment*, 335.
153. Kant, *Critique of Practical Reason*, 102.

practical reason."[154] His understanding of morality is characterized by a distinctively Christian form of *eudaimonism*, the philosophical doctrine that happiness is the highest end of moral
good. He stresses that there is no true happiness apart from the
"holiness of morals."[155] He even comes close to the tradition of
the Westminster Catechisms when he states in parallel fashion:
(1) "God's final end in creating the world . . . [is] the happiness
of the rational beings in . . . the highest good"; (2) "those who
put the end of creation in the glory of God . . . perhaps hit upon
the best expression."[156]

Still, in the foregoing analysis, we must note that Kant differs
fundamentally from the Westminster tradition in particular and
traditional Christianity in general in two important and related
respects. First, as far as the second *Critique* is concerned, the
historical person and work of Jesus Christ is entirely irrelevant
to Kant's understanding of enjoying and glorifying God. The
Christocentrism of the Reformed doctrine of the covenants is
foreign to Kant's philosophy. Second, Kant's rational faith in God
explicitly excludes "historical" faith, which really "would have to
be called credulity and not faith."[157] Yet the exclusion of credulity
does not amount to skepticism, which is as irrational as credulity.
To be "incredulous," which "means to stick to the maxim not to
believe testimony at all," is not a mark of true faith either, for true
faith is rational.[158]

God as Supreme Moral Legislator

Kant is emphatic that faith in Christian doctrine has to
be rational, rather than dogmatic. Rational faith in Christian

---

154. Kant, *Critique of Practical Reason*, 102.
155. Kant, *Critique of Practical Reason*, 102.
156. Kant, *Critique of Practical Reason*, 105.
157. Kant, *Critique of the Power of Judgment*, 335.
158. Kant, *Critique of the Power of Judgment*, 336.

doctrine constitutes true religion; credulity toward the historical testimonies of the Scriptures gives rise to groundless dogmatics. It is "only with religion that the *hope* of happiness first arises."[159] Faith and hope go hand in hand. Now the question remains: "What may I hope?"

For Kant, hope is an intrinsically religious and theological matter—it is a matter of faith. The famous first sentence of the conclusion to the second *Critique* appears to be an anticipation of how he would set out to answer the question of hope in the third *Critique*: "Two things fill the mind with ever new and increasing admiration and reverence [*Erfurcht*], the more often and more steadily one *reflects* on them: the starry heavens above me and the moral law within me."[160]

In the third *Critique*, Kant introduces the notion of the *reflecting* (*reflektierend*) use of the faculty of the *power of judgment* (*Urteilskraft*). When we judge something to be beautiful, sublime, or good, we exercise the power of judgment. In the reflecting use of this power, we are given something particular, such as the starry heavens, and then we work our way up to a universal under which the particular may be subsumed. When we reflect upon the "starry heavens," a feeling of awe or reverence is aroused, and we call "the sight . . . **sublime.**"[161]

Aesthetic judgments pertain mainly to two kinds of objects: the beautiful and the sublime. *The beautiful* (*das Schöne*) gives rise to an immediate feeling of pleasure, and it "pleases without [subjective] interest," for it is a symbol of the moral good.[162] When I call *Mona Lisa* beautiful, it is because it carries certain artistic forms—perspective, colors, lighting, etc.—that immediately please me. The beautiful does not please my senses—I do

159. Kant, *Critique of Practical Reason*, 105 (italics original).
160. Kant, *Critique of Practical Reason*, 129 (italics added).
161. Kant, *Critique of the Power of Judgment*, 152 (boldface original).
162. Kant, *Critique of the Power of Judgment*, 227.

not really sense beauty as an empirical object—nor does it please "in accordance with a concept of the understanding," for the feeling of the beautiful is immediate.[163] The pleasure associated with the beautiful is purely positive.

The sublime (das Erhabene), on the other hand, arouses a feeling of satisfaction that is "only negative": it is a "feeling of the deprivation of the freedom of the imagination by itself," characterized by "astonishment bordering on terror, the horror and the awesome shudder, which grip the spectator in viewing mountain ranges towering to the heavens, deep ravines and the raging torrents in them, deeply shadowed wastelands inducing melancholy reflection, etc."[164] The sublime as such "pleases *immediately*" as well, albeit "through its *resistance* to the interest of the senses," whereas the beautiful only pleases without interest.[165] In the presence of the sublime, we feel something greater than life, as it were—a cause that subjects us to "sacrifice" and willing "deprivation."[166]

Both the starry heavens above me and the moral law within me are sublime. Both occasion our rational faith in God: the "physical teleology" of nature "gives our theoretically reflecting power of judgment a sufficient basis for assuming the existence of an intelligent world-cause," while "we also find in ourselves ... a moral teleology" that points us to God as the supreme moral agent.[167]

The main body of the third *Critique* is primarily preoccupied with the sublime in nature—such as the starry heavens and towering mountain ranges. What Kant calls "the sublimity [*Erhabenheit*] and inner dignity" of the moral law is discussed mainly in the

---

163. Kant, *Critique of the Power of Judgment*, 150.
164. Kant, *Critique of the Power of Judgment*, 151.
165. Kant, *Critique of the Power of Judgment*, 150 (italics added).
166. Kant, *Critique of the Power of Judgment*, 151.
167. Kant, *Critique of the Power of Judgment*, 313.

final appendix, titled "Methodology of the Teleological Power of Judgment," which comprises a modified version of the central theological thesis stated in the second *Critique.*

Moving beyond the *Groundwork* and the second *Critique,* Kant now conceptually identifies God as not only the supreme determining ground of our moral will, but also "the highest morally legislative author."[168] God is still considered an object of faith, not knowledge. Faith is, by definition, rational. The rationality of faith in God as the supreme moral legislator lies in this: "*given* the constitution of the faculty of our reason, we could not even make comprehensible the kind of purposiveness related to the moral law and its object that exists in this final end without an author and ruler of the world who is at the same time a moral legislator."[169]

While the unequivocal identification of God as supreme moral legislator is an important breakthrough, the third *Critique* remains unsatisfactory for Kant in several ways. One chief problem is that both its arrangement and its contents fall short of answering the question of hope that it is intended to answer. The reason is that *hope* is a soteriological notion: we hope to be saved from a certain plight that we desire to escape. More precisely, hope is occasioned by the need of grace as divine assistance. The sublimity of creation does not occasion our need of salvific grace. It is the moral sublime that invokes our awareness of this need. By devoting the main body of the third *Critique* to the beautiful and the sublime in relation to freedom, the soteriological question of hope is largely left out of sight. Even in the theological appendix, soteric grace plays only a peripheral role.

Kant's sporadic discussions of hope in the third *Critique* are mainly about happiness associated with moral action, and

168. Kant, *Critique of the Power of Judgment,* 320.
169. Kant, *Critique of the Power of Judgment,* 320 (italics added).

sometimes about a future life (the metaphysical idea of the immortality of the soul). These do not satisfactorily address the great philosophical question of hope. A number of building blocks have emerged in this *Critique,* but the edifice has yet to be built. For instance, how is the deeply theological notion of *sacrifice,* associated with the sublime in the third *Critique,* related to the soteriological question of *hope?* The elements of sacrifice, atonement, and hope remain unconnected in the third *Critique.*

Some commentators have pointed out that the theological appendix to the third *Critique* is reflective of Kant's own dissatisfaction with the work's failure to accomplish its purpose of answering the question of hope. Palmquist puts it well: "even with this Appendix . . . , the third *Critique* provided an incomplete and only partially successful explanation of how human hope arises at the intersection of nature and freedom. The need for a more complete answer to the question of hope drove Kant to devote his next major work to a Critical philosophy of religion."[170] It is in *Religion* that Kant finally fills in the theological core of his moral philosophy and gives a mature—though still problematic— answer to the question of hope in divine grace.

Hope in God's Assistance

Chronologically, *Religion* is the first of Kant's major works after the three *Critiques.* A number of English translations are available, but Werner Pluhar's is the only one that offers a correct rendering of the title. The German word *bloß* in the original title has been variously rendered as "pure," "mere," and "alone." The first is simply wrong: *pure* (*rein*) means "*a priori* and unadulterated with experience," which is clearly different from *bloß.* The connotations of *alone* have given "rise to a disastrous tendency to read Kantian religion as moral reductionism" in the Anglophone

---

170. Palmquist, "Introduction," in Kant, *Religion,* xx.

literature—a point that we will explain in a moment.[171] While *bloß* does connote *mere*, it does not encapsulate its intended meaning: in the preface to *Religion*, Kant likens rational religion to a naked body that needs to be clothed by historical doctrines.

Kant envisions pure religion and biblical revelation as two concentric circles. Biblical faith is the outer circle, peripheral to the inner circle of pure rational faith. This picture is meant to convey the point that if one obeys the precepts of the Bible, one would also be an observer of the moral precepts of pure reason. One can still be a member of the moral kingdom of ends, however, without being a member of the Christian church and accepting biblical revelation as one's personal faith.

In fact, Kant acknowledges the Bible as divine revelation, but he downplays its historical dimension, which he thinks is fraught with contingencies and inconsistencies—both internal inconsistencies and inconsistencies with the moral law of pure reason. Still, he thinks that pure religion is not derived from reason alone: the translation of *bloß* as "alone" is highly problematic, precisely because it suggests that for Kant, pure religion is the same as morality, which can be derived from reason alone, without divine revelation.

Pure religion is not based only on the idea of revelation: it is necessarily based on historical revelation as a vehicle that emulates pure religion. As Kant himself puts it in his later work *The Metaphysics of Morals* (1797), pure religion "is not . . . derived from reason alone but is also based on the teachings of history and revelation, and considers only the harmony of pure practical reason with these."[172] Human reason alone is a naked body.

---

171. Palmquist, "Introduction," in Kant, *Religion*, xv.

172. Immanuel Kant, *The Metaphysics of Morals*, ed. and trans. Mary Gregor (Cambridge: Cambridge University Press, 1991), 276. See John Hare's comment on this quote: John Hare, *The Moral Gap: Kantian Ethics, Human Limits, and God's Assistance* (Oxford: Oxford University Press, 1996), 40n4.

It remains hopeless if it is not clothed with God's grace and revelation.

The central claim of *Religion* is that "morality . . . leads inescapably to religion, through which it expands to the idea of a powerful moral legislator, outside the human being, in whose will the final purpose (of the world's creation) is that which at the same time *can be*, and *ought to be*, the final purpose of the human being."[173] This combination of the *can be* (theoretical reason) and *ought to be* (practical reason) was the intention of Kant's third *Critique*, which, as we saw, did not succeed in elevating moral philosophy to the level of religion, in which alone soteric hope can be found.

Religion is unmistakably soteriological. Kant describes humanity's salvation from its plight of evil as "the restoration . . . of the *purity* of the moral law as the supreme basis of all our maxims," and the moral law "after that restoration . . . not merely as linked with other incentives . . . , but rather in its entire purity as incentive *sufficient* by itself for determining the power of choice."[174]

Humanity is evil in its natural propensity in three respects. First, the human heart is weak in "complying with adopted maxims"; second, human beings have the "propensity to mix immoral incentives with the moral"; and third, human beings are "wicked" in the "propensity to adopt evil maxims."[175] These propensities are not coercive with respect to human choice. Rather, human beings carry out these propensities intelligently and willfully, that is, in (negative) freedom. Only thus can human beings be held guilty for their sins.

Moreover, there is an "original moral *predisposition* within us," and it is the "moral vocation" for all humans to restore in

173. Kant, *Metaphysics of Morals*, 4 (italics added).
174. Kant, *Metaphysics of Morals*, 52 (italics original).
175. Kant, *Metaphysics of Morals*, 32.

our maxims the original moral good.[176] Here Kant retrieves an important notion developed in the third *Critique* and attaches it supremely to morality: he emphasizes the utmost importance of the "repeated arousing of [the] feeling of the *sublimity* of one's moral calling."[177] The gap between the "dignity and sublimity" of the moral law within us, of which Kant speaks in the *Groundwork,* and the faculty of judgment with our capability of feeling, which he discusses at length in the third *Critique,* is thus bridged in *Religion.*

Note that Kant distinguishes between our natural *propensity to evil* (*Hang zum Bösen*) and *predisposition to the good* (*Anlage zum Guten*). This is roughly in line with the Latin Christian doctrine of original sin, according to which human beings are good by essential nature, and became sinful in acquiring an accidental nature through the fall. Kant states that "the human being . . . is created good," in the sense that "he is created for the *good,* and the original *predisposition* in the human being is good."[178]

A *predisposition* is an innate property that cannot be extinguished, whereas a propensity can "be thought (if it is good) as *acquired,* or (if it is evil) as *brought upon* the human being by himself."[179] Kant defines *propensity* as "the subjective basis for the possibility of an inclination (habitual desire . . .) insofar as this possibility is contingent for humanity as such."[180] This distinction serves to support his view that human beings must be held responsible for adopting evil maxims in their evil propensities through the negative freedom of *choice* (*Willkür*). Kant's definition of *propensity* as something accidental to human nature also serves to underscore his final aim in moral religion, namely, a

176. Kant, *Metaphysics of Morals,* 56–57 (italics added).
177. Kant, *Metaphysics of Morals,* 57 (italics added).
178. Kant, *Metaphysics of Morals,* 50 (italics original).
179. Kant, *Metaphysics of Morals,* 31 (italics original).
180. Kant, *Metaphysics of Morals,* 31.

conscious turning away from evil propensities and the subordination of natural propensities to the moral law in one's maxims and actions.

Kant identifies the adoption of "self-love . . . as the principle of all our maxims" as "precisely the source of all evil."[181] Echoing Martin Luther, Kant states that the initiation of recovery from evil to the good in one's habits requires "not exactly a change of heart, but only a change of mores."[182] Citing John 3:5 with reference to Genesis 1:2, Kant states that the "change of heart" as "a kind of rebirth, as if through a new creation," is subsequent and not antecedent to the change of mores.[183] The change of heart as "a *revolution* in the attitude in the human being"—"a transition to the maxim of the attitude's holiness"—however, is necessary for the fulfillment of our moral vocation.[184]

The problem is that in view of the frailty, impurity, and wickedness of human nature, it is beyond human capacity to undergo the change of heart. We need the grace of God for salvation from evil. But whence our hope in God's grace? Kant cites Luke 19:12–16 and argues that if a human being "has employed his original predisposition to the good in order to become a better human being, [he] can . . . hope that what is not in his capacity will be compensated for by a higher cooperation."[185]

Kant does not offer any theoretical ground for this hope. Rather, our hope for divine assistance is grounded in practical faith, that is, what we may rationally believe when we reflect on what we ought to do. A human being ought to "do as much as is in his powers in order to become a better human being."[186] We

---

181. Kant, *Metaphysics of Morals*, 51.
182. Kant, *Metaphysics of Morals*, 53. See editor's note on Luther's doctrine, n252.
183. Kant, *Metaphysics of Morals*, 53.
184. Kant, *Metaphysics of Morals*, 53 (italics original).
185. Kant, *Metaphysics of Morals*, 59.
186. Kant, *Metaphysics of Morals*, 59.

may and should hope for divine compensation for moral imperfections, because without God's grace, there is no way to fathom the possibility of fulfilling our sublime moral vocation.

We ought to hope for grace because this hope prevents us from giving up on the moral quest and encourages us to progress morally. "'It is not essential and therefore not necessary for everyone to know what God does, or has done, for his salvation,' but it certainly is essential and is necessary for everyone to know *what the human being himself has to do* in order to become worthy of this assistance."[187]

In this way, Kant's moral religion downplays the historical nature of the atonement. The *pro nobis*—"for us and for our salvation"—in our creeds is reduced in Kant to practical faith detached from knowledge. We ought to hope, even if we do not know what God has done or does for us and for our salvation.

The difficulty is, even granted that one can hope to be delivered from the plight of evil at some future point in one's life, how can one atone for one's past guilt? It is crucial to note that Kant himself identifies the problem of the atonement as the "greatest difficulty" of his moral religion: "Whatever may have happened in [a human being's] case with the adoption of a good attitude, and indeed, however persistently he continues in this attitude in a way of life conforming to it, *he yet started from evil*, and this indebtedness it will never be possible for him to erase."[188] In other words, how is the remission of sins possible in a purely moral religion?

In proposing a solution to this problem, Kant finds his starting point in the Reformation's understanding of human guilt or "original debt" as moral guilt that deserves punishment.[189] The Reformers, while building on Anselm's satisfaction theory of the

---

187. Kant, *Metaphysics of Morals*, 59 (italics original).
188. Kant, *Metaphysics of Morals*, 80 (italics original).
189. Kant, *Metaphysics of Morals*, 80.

atonement, insist that the Anselmian understanding of satisfaction of divine justice is far from sufficient to atone for humanity's sin, because the debt that humanity owes God, as Kant puts it, "is not a *transmissible* obligation . . . like . . . a monetary debt . . . , but is the *most personal of all* obligations, namely a debt of sins, which only the punishable one can bear, not the innocent one."[190] In other words, there can be no satisfaction of the supreme justice without proper punishment of the subject of sin. Kant insists that "satisfaction must be rendered to the highest justice, before which someone punishable can never go unpunished."[191]

While this may sound especially agreeable to readers who subscribe to the Reformed doctrines of justification and the atonement, Kant deviates fundamentally from the Protestant understanding of penal substitution. Whereas the Reformers, in line with Anselm, assert that human sin carries infinite guilt because of the infinity of the party offended (namely, God), Kant maintains that "moral evil carries with it an *infinity* of violations of the law and hence an infinity of guilt, not so much because of the infinity of the supreme legistator, whose authority has thereby been violated . . . , but as an evil in the *attitude* and the maxims as such (like *universal principles* as contrasted with individual transgressions)."[192]

Note that Kant is careful to say that the infinity of human guilt is "*not so much* because of" God's infinity. He does not completely negate God's infinity as the ground of our offense. To say that our violation of God's authority constitutes an infinite guilt is to assert "an extravagant relation of the human being to the supreme being, *of which we understand nothing*."[193] Our guilt is infinite because the moral law is universal. Better put, because

190. Kant, *Metaphysics of Morals*, 80 (italics original).
191. Kant, *Metaphysics of Morals*, 81.
192. Kant, *Metaphysics of Morals*, 80 (italics original).
193. Kant, *Metaphysics of Morals*, 80 (italics added).

the moral law is universal, the evil maxims that we adopt against the moral law are universal in scope, which somehow translates to the infinity of our guilt.

How universality translates to infinity is not at all clear in Kant's text. In any case, he maintains that "moral evil carries with it this infinity of violations and of guilt," and so "every human being would have to expect an *infinite punishment* and expulsion from the kingdom of God."[194] Atonement is crucial if we are to participate in God's kingdom, the moral kingdom of ends. Yet the person and work of Jesus Christ, in their historical dimension, cannot provide genuine atonement. Atonement is a matter of faith, and faith is a matter of reason. There is an unbridgeable gulf between contingent matters of fact and the necessary truths of reason. The historicity of Christ's death makes this event a contingent matter of fact, and so it cannot be an object of rational faith. Moreover, rational faith does not admit of credulity toward testimonies. How, then, is the atonement possible?

Kant proposes a rational "solution" to the problem of the atonement.[195] In short, it states that "the exit from the corrupted into the good attitude . . . is in itself already a sacrifice and an entrance upon a long series of life's ills that the new human being takes upon himself in the attitude of the Son of God— in other words, merely for the sake of the good—but that yet were properly deserved by a [morally] different human being, namely the old one, as *punishment.*"[196] In other words, the sacrifice of happiness associated with the endeavors to live a moral life constitutes the very punishment that the sinner deserves. Paradoxically, it is through this sacrifice of happiness that one attains true happiness. The very sublimity of the moral vocation lies in this requirement of sacrifice. The feeling of pleasure

194. Kant, *Metaphysics of Morals*, 80 (italics added).
195. Kant, *Metaphysics of Morals*, 81.
196. Kant, *Metaphysics of Morals*, 83 (italics original).

associated with the sublime differs from that associated with the beautiful, precisely in that the sublime pleases by requiring sacrifice.

Moving on, Kant employs a series of theological expressions that bear formal resemblance to the Reformed understanding of salvation and the atonement. He begins the discourse by describing a union with the Son of God.[197] But his understanding of union with Christ—and indeed all the traditional theological and biblical expressions he employs—is merely metaphoric and symbolic. While Reformed theology speaks of a mystical union by faith, Kant, remaining within his own bounds of bare reason, proposes the idea of a union of attitudes.[198]

The attitude is something that we can feel, something within our power of judgment. The attitude of the Son is an attitude of sacrifice in association with the sublimity of our moral vocation. On this basis, Kant speaks allegorically of penal substitution, imputation, satisfaction, and justification in a long sentence spanning two pages:

> And this attitude in its purity, like the purity of the Son of God which he has admitted into himself, or (if we personify this idea) *the latter* himself, as *proxy*, bears for him, and thus also for all who have (practical) faith in him, the debt of sins; renders satisfaction, as *redeemer*, to the highest justice through suffering and death; and brings it about, as *advocate*, that they can hope to appear before their judge as justified, except that . . . the suffering which the new human being must continually take upon himself in his life while dying unto the *old* human being is conceived in the representative of humankind as a death suffered once and for all.—Here, then, is that surplus beyond the

197. Kant, *Metaphysics of Morals*, 83.
198. Kant, *Metaphysics of Morals*, 83.

merit of works that earlier we were unable to find, and it is a merit that is imputed to us *by grace*.[199]

Note Kant's comments in the parentheses above: he employs these theological expressions as metaphoric personification. Biblical testimonies and ecclesial dogmas are important for clothing the naked body of pure reason, but they should not be understood literally. They lead to practical-rational faith in moral-religious truths only if they are taken allegorically.

This faith is not just a personal matter. Because of the universality of the moral vocation, a moral-religious community on earth must be its final end. Kant thus proceeds from the basis of soteriology to develop an ecclesiology that depicts his vision of the true church as the kingdom of God in the form of an ethical community on earth. He describes the true church as both invisible ("a bare idea, of the union of all righteous persons under the divine direct") and visible ("actual union of human beings to form a whole that harmonizes with that ideal").[200]

The pure religious faith that characterizes the true church is moral and pertains to practical reason. This rational faith within the bounds of bare reason can be communicated to all humans because moral reason is universal. It is as such not a historical faith based on factual claims (e.g., Christ's resurrection). For Kant, this means that the pure religious faith of the true church cannot be revelational in essence, since revelation is historical and not universal.

Yet as noted earlier, Kant does not intend to dispense with statutory church faith. For him, revealed faith is an inevitable vehicle for emulating pure moral faith. Pure rational religion is necessarily clothed with empirical, historical religion (i.e.,

---

199. Kant, *Metaphysics of Morals*, 83–85 (italics original).
200. Kant, *Metaphysics of Morals*, 128.

Christianity). "Historical faith . . . cannot be authenticated," while "the pure faith of reason . . . does not need any such authentication, but proves itself."[201]

Empirical religion is merely the means, while pure rational religion is its end. For this reason, Scriptures, though important, should be subjected to moral-rational faith. Church faith has pure religious faith as its highest interpreter, and so forced or allegorical interpretations are to be preferred over literal readings of the Scriptures. After all, the final aim of reading the Scriptures and formulating doctrines is to make better human beings. Kant suggests that "historical faith" as a vehicle to "emulate pure religion" must at the end be dispensed with, when it has accomplished its purpose.[202] Then the church militant will become the church triumphant.

Cloaked under these theological metaphors is Kant's vision of an "ethically civil society," in contrast to a "juridically civil society."[203] Ideally, the state should play a minimal role in its legislative and judicial functions. In an ethically civil society, all members freely participate in universal-moral legislation. They are not coerced by the laws of the state to behave ethically. Morally good behavior under coercion has no dignity. Dignity lies in autonomy, and autonomy presupposes freedom from coercion.

Before such a society is established on earth, paternalistic state powers may be necessary. Legalism, however, will not ultimately succeed in fulfilling our sublime moral vocation. If the dignity and sublimity of the supreme moral law within us are to shine forth at all, we must have faith and hope in God's assistance.

If there is any traditional theological expression in *Religion* that is meant to be taken literally, it would be the notion of divine assistance. That is, Kant really envisions God's assistance as an

201. Kant, *Metaphysics of Morals*, 143–44.
202. Kant, *Metaphysics of Morals*, 127.
203. Kant, *Metaphysics of Morals*, 103.

act of God that is supernatural and *extra nos*. This is not to say that the entire section on this notion (Second Piece, Section One) is composed of literal expressions. In this section, Kant presents the notion of divine assistance as a triune economy, but the persons of the Trinity are not understood in line with the traditional dogma of the church. Professor John Hare puts it well when he describes Kant's effort as a "translation project": Kant is experimenting with translating traditional Christian dogmas into the universal moral precepts of pure religion.[204]

In Kant's translation of the triune economy, the Father is represented as the universal idea of holiness; the Son, as morally perfected humanity; and the Holy Spirit, our Comforter, as our good *attitude* (*Gesinnung*)—a Kantian notion that is difficult to pin down (and we will not bother to explain it here).[205] Yet we have to understand that Kant is speaking of the triune economy as only God's works on our behalf here. He is not reducing God to a mere tripartite moral ideal. He literally believes that God exists as a moral and intelligent agent, and that God works on our behalf to accomplish what is beyond our capabilities.

Any secularist attempt to interpretively naturalize or allegorize the notion of divine assistance in Kant would render Kantian ethics meaningless, for the whole edifice of Kantian ethics stands or falls with this plank. Professor Hare observes that in Kant's system, "ought . . . implies can."[206] If salvation from sin is impossible by our own efforts, the only hope that it can be achieved is that God works on our behalf. But because by pure reason we know that we ought to be saved from sin, we must hope and assume, by faith, that God will literally help us, for without divine assistance we are doomed to fail. If we do not take God's

204. Hare, *Moral Gap*, 60.
205. For an in-depth discussion of *Gesinnung*, see Julia Peters, "Kant's *Gesinnung*," *Journal of the History of Philosophy* 56, 3 (2018): 497–518.
206. Hare, *Moral Gap*, 35.

assistance literally, then the *ought to* ceases to be meaningful. Kant would then be wrong about the universality and sublimity of our moral vocation. He would also be wrong in asserting that every human being is endowed with an intrinsic and invaluable core that he calls *dignity*.

But the questions remain: apart from saving faith in the historical person and work of Jesus Christ, and the economy of the triune God as revealed in the Bible, can we secure any hope of God's assistance for ourselves? Without knowing the righteous and loving God whose wrath cannot be appeased without the execution of his judgment, either in our own persons or in the person of the Son, can we make sense of the trembling feeling of horror that Kant associates with the sublime? If the creation-fall-redemption triad is taken allegorically, without a literally Christ-centered understanding, can we identify any meaning or purpose in history? These are questions that we will consider in the next chapter.

3

A REFORMED ASSESSMENT
OF KANT'S THOUGHT

Theology as Science:
Kant and Modern Christian Thought

In the previous chapter, we saw that the Critical question, what we as human beings can and cannot know, undergirds Kant's philosophy as a whole. He was driven by the concern to safeguard science, morality, and religion from the threat of empiricist skepticism that resulted from the rationalist philosophy of knowing it all. At the heart of both empiricism and rationalism was a theory of ideas that was egotistic and subjectivistic to its core. In his attempt to secure the objectivity of science and morality, he had to "deny knowledge in order to make room for faith."[1] This severance of faith from knowledge led to one of the deepest problems driving the developments of modern Christian

1. Immanuel Kant, *Critique of Pure Reason*, ed. and trans. Paul Guyer and Allen Wood (Cambridge: Cambridge University Press, 2007), Bxxx.

thought: how can theology be scientific? That is, how can human beings attain theoretical knowledge of God?

Because of the centrality of this Kantian problem to nineteenth-century Christian thought, Kant has often been described as "the great watershed figure" between early-modern and modern theology.[2] Bruce McCormack, renowned scholar of modern theology, aptly comments that "it was the rise of 'historical consciousness'—by which I mean the awareness that all human thinking is conditioned by historical (and cultural) location—that was most basic to the emergence of what we tend to think of as 'modern' theology today."[3] He explains that the "first" of the "most significant preconditions necessary for the emergence of historical consciousness as a culturewide phenomenon in Germany" was "Kant's limitation of what may be known by the theoretical reason in phenomenal reality."[4] This resonates with Karl Ameriks's authoritative narration of the "historical turn" of European thought and culture in modernity, which began with "a stage-setting Kantian prehistory," followed by the "early post-Kantian 'founder's era.'"[5]

It is important for us to understand Kant's role as a stage-setting, rather than founding, figure of modern theology. Ascribing this role to him allows us to define the term *modern*, not with a definite set of presuppositions, but rather with a set of characteristically modern problems related to the "historical turn" after him. Different theologians tackled these problems with different sets of presuppositions. This is the sense in

2. Joel Rasmussen, "The Transformation of Metaphysics," in *The Oxford Handbook of Nineteenth-Century Christian Thought*, ed. Joel Rasmussen, Judith Wolfe, and Johannes Zachhuber (Oxford: Oxford University Press, 2017), 12.

3. Bruce McCormack, *Orthodox and Modern: Studies in the Theology of Karl Barth* (Grand Rapids: Baker, 2008), 10–11.

4. McCormack, *Orthodox and Modern*, 11.

5. Karl Ameriks, *Kant and the Historical Turn: Philosophy as Critical Interpretation* (Oxford: Oxford University Press, 2006), 15.

which Cory Brock, for instance, can describe Herman Bavinck as "orthodox yet modern."[6]

Underlying this set of problems is the aforementioned question of the scientific status of theology. One implication of Kant's critique of knowledge is that what we inevitably think we know about innate metaphysical ideas such as God is merely an illusion, as far as the theoretical use of reason is concerned. In the practical use of reason, to be sure, ideas such as God become immanent to us, but as we saw in chapter 2, the postulation of these metaphysical ideas is practical, rather than theoretical. We know that *God ought to be*, but we cannot claim to know, as a matter of fact, that *God is*.

Kant, to be sure, does occasionally describe what he calls *transcendental theology* and even *biblical theology* as sciences. Strictly speaking, however, as Professor Stephen Palmquist reminds us, Kant has "barred human beings from all scientific [by which Palmquist means *theoretical*: practical knowledge can also be scientific in some sense] *knowledge* of God."[7] G. W. F. Hegel (1770–1831) is right, notwithstanding his overall misinterpretation of Kant, that speculative metaphysics and theology in his time had been "extirpated root and branch, and [had] vanished from the ranks of the sciences," because of "Kantian philosophy."[8]

More precisely, Kant's transcendental idealism dictates that human *scientia* is formally confined by spatiotemporality. Science as systematized theoretical knowledge must involve some combination of empirical observations of objects of experience with

6. See Cory Brock, "Orthodox yet Modern: Herman Bavinck's Appropriation of Schleiermacher" (PhD thesis, University of Edinburgh, 2018).

7. Stephen R. Palmquist, "Introduction," in Immanuel Kant, *Religion within the Bounds of Bare Reason*, trans. Werner S. Pluhar (Indianapolis: Hackett, 2009), xix (emphasis original).

8. Georg Wilhelm Friedrich Hegel, *The Science of Logic*, ed. and trans. George di Giovanni (Cambridge: Cambridge University Press, 2010), 7–8.

conceptual necessities inherent to our intellect and reason. Because our minds can process only sensory data perceived through space and time, our knowledge is limited to what is phenomenal and historical.

God, professes the Christian, transcends space and time as the one who created space and time out of nothing. How can the infinite and timeless essence of God, then, become an object of human knowledge? How can theology as the systematic study of God be a science? This is in fact a question that Christian theology has considered since its very inception in the earliest Old Testament periods, when the saints marveled at the name of Yahweh whom no creature could name. But it came sharply to the foreground with distinctively modern rigor after Kant.

Abraham Kuyper (1837–1920), at around the turn of the twentieth century, paints in his characteristically broad strokes an accurate picture:

> Impelled by its own exceptional position, as well as by the alarming attitude the other sciences assumed against it, Theology was the first to give itself an account of its place and of its calling. For the greater part of the last century, however, this attempt bore an apologetic character; and only when by and after Kant the question about the essence and the method of our knowledge, and consequently of the nature of science in general, pressed itself forcefully to the front, in our human consciousness, was there gradually adopted the organic interpretation of Theology as a whole and as one of the sciences in the great unit of the sciences . . . . Formerly a science of Theology in that sense was not necessary . . . ; neither was it possible.[9]

---

9. Abraham Kuyper, *Encyclopedia of Sacred Theology: Its Principles* (New York: Scribner's, 1898), 293.

Aside from the orthodox yet modern answers to the problem of the scientific status of theology after Kant offered by theologians such as Kuyper, Charles Hodge (1797–1878), and Herman Bavinck (1854–1921), there have been at least three other basic approaches in the modern period of theology. The so-called Right Hegelians found an ally in Hegel in reacting against Kant, seeking to secure the systematic nature of the science of theology by integrating Hegel's metaphysical system with Protestant orthodoxies. Another approach, of which Søren Kierkegaard (1813–55) is representative, stressed the subjectivity of faith. Kierkegaard argued, with Kant, that Christianity is inherently "unscientific." On this basis, Kierkegaard refused to systematize the Christian faith within the secular enterprise of modern science.[10]

The most influential approach within nineteenth-century Protestantism in Europe, as far as academic theology is concerned, was the historicization of the discipline in the wake of Kant's critique of scientific knowledge. At the core of this general approach is the theological historicism to which post-Kantian idealism gave rise. *Historicism*, in simple terms, is a philosophical way of seeing history as purposive activity. A famous proponent

10. It must be clarified that in the field of Kierkegaard studies, the basic consensus is that it is a mistake to label the Danish thinker as a *fideist* or *irrationalist*. His opposition of Christianity to science and culture has been widely misunderstood outside the field of Kierkegaard studies in this respect. He is opposed to *rationality* and *science* only as defined in modern rationalistic terms. In fact, he insists that the apparent contradictions of Christian doctrines are results of the noetic effects of sin. See Joel Rasmussen, *Between Irony and Witness: Kierkegaard's Poetics of Faith, Hope, and Love* (London: T&T Clark, 2005), 93–95. For a discussion of Kierkegaard and culture, see my "Kierkegaard and Music in Paradox? Bringing Mozart's *Don Giovanni* to Terms with Kierkegaard's Religious Life-View," *Literature and Theology* 28, 4 (2014): 411–24. Professor John Hare has identified a deeply Kantian core in Kierkegaard's thought, which shows that the labels of *fideism* and *irrationalism* are indeed misused. See John Hare, *The Moral Gap: Kantian Ethics, Human Limits, and God's Assistance* (Oxford: Oxford University Press, 1996).

of this approach is Ferdinand Christian Baur (1792–1860), founder of the New Tübingen School. He applied Hegel's dialectical view of history to historical theology and biblical studies.

One early post-Kantian idealist often considered the founder of this historicist approach is Friedrich Schleiermacher (1768–1834).[11] Kuyper, who is severely critical of Schleiermacher, credits Schleiermacher, *inter alia*, with being the "first theologian in the higher scientific sense" after Kant.[12] Often called (in rather oversimplified manners) the father of a loosely defined brand of theology variously dubbed "liberal," "modernist," "neo-Protestant," and that of "modern consciousness," Schleiermacher reacted to Kant by turning theology into a *historical* science.

This has to do with Kant's critique of historical religion. He argues that statutory faith of the Christian churches holds to revealed doctrines, but that revelation is historical, rather than universal (see chapter 2). This means that the particular events of history that Christian dogmas and Scriptures purport to report cannot be universally communicated as knowledge. Moral reason, on the other hand, is universal—it can be universally communicated, albeit as rational faith, rather than knowledge. Kant himself matriculated at the University of Königsberg as a student of theology, and supported throughout his life the government's efforts in promoting theological studies at institutions of higher learning. The overall result of his views, however, placed theology in urgent need of justifying its right of residence within higher academia.

Schleiermacher saw himself as a defender of the theological science. His strategy was to first concede to Kant that Christian dogmas are indeed historical in nature. Christian dogmatics as such must, in Kantian terms, reason practically (*what ought to be*),

11. Johannes Zachhuber, "The Historical Turn," in *Oxford Handbook of Nineteenth-Century Christian Thought*, 57.

12. Kuyper, *Encyclopedia*, 675.

rather than theoretically (*what is*). "For Schleiermacher, the task of dogmatics is to answer the question, 'What must *be*, given the reality of Christian self-consciousness?'"[13]

With Kant, Schleiermacher reinvented traditional Christian doctrines as expressions of natural historical processes. The traditional doctrine of the Trinity and the two-nature Christology of Chalcedonian orthodoxy are, for Schleiermacher, "beyond what persons can legitimately know."[14] Thus, Schleiermacher espoused a form of religious naturalism. He, like Kant, reduced the supernatural dimension of his theology to the very minimum: "the one remaining 'supernatural' element in Schleiermacher's otherwise seamlessly 'naturalistic' system'" is the idea of Jesus as the "perfection of humanity" with "perfect . . . God-consciousness."[15]

From his Kantian starting points, however, Schleiermacher moved beyond Kant. Kant believed in the universality of true religion, but Schleiermacher insisted that we should focus on the particularity of the essence of religion, which he identified as the *feeling* (*Gefühl*) of absolute dependence on God. Positive religion (Christianity and Judaism) is superior to natural religion (deism), primarily because of the former's historical particularity in expressing this feeling. According to the later Schleiermacher, this is a feeling of the need of redemption. He even claims that "salvation or blessedness is in the Church alone."[16] This is because it is only within the natural-historical phenomena of the faith and life of the church expressed through historic dogmas

13. James Brandt, *All Things New: Reform of Church and Society in Schleiermacher's Christian Ethics* (Louisville: Westminster John Knox, 2001), 90, quoting Friedrich Schleiermacher, *Die christliche Sitte*, ed. Ludwig Jonas, in *Sämmtliche Werke*, 1.12 (Berlin: Reimer, 1843), 23 (italics original).

14. Brandt, *All Things New*, 38.

15. Brandt, *All Things New*, 38.

16. Friedrich Schleiermacher, *The Christian Faith*, trans. H. R. Mackintosh and J. S. Stewart (London: T&T Clark, 1928), 527.

that "the result of His [the Redeemer's] personal influence" becomes "veritable."[17]

Dogmatics as such, per Schleiermacher, is the historical study of Christian dogmas as particular, culturally conditioned expressions of humanity's consciousness of God. Concomitantly, biblical studies should be a hermeneutical science (i.e., of textual interpretation) that has as its object of inquiry not so much the supernatural God of the Scriptures, but rather the biblical texts as historically conditioned expressions of natural human God-consciousness.

In this way, Schleiermacher gave rise to the basic approach of the diverse and complex tradition of modern liberal theology. His defense of the academic status of the theological science was overwhelmingly successful within the scholarly guild. We should also acknowledge that his intention was not to reduce theology to a nonmetaphysical science, or to maintain that theology is not concerned with knowledge of God. Still, in Schleiermacher, the scientific aspect of theology is limited to its study of history, while the God of history is only indirectly reflected through our study of history.

We should applaud Schleiermacher for his desire to safeguard our knowledge of Christ as God incarnate, but his rejection of traditional two-nature Christology is destructive to his very own intention. In the confines of Kant's critique of metaphysics, idealist metaphysicians of Schleiermacher's generation were convinced that human beings within the temporal world cannot claim knowledge of the proposition *God is*.

Post-Kantian idealists were not satisfied with confining theology to practical reason (*God ought to be*), however. Thus, they moved beyond Kant—upon Kantian presuppositions—in asserting that human knowledge is confined to events and

17. Schleiermacher, *Christian Faith*, 385, 526.

activities—to *becoming*. The Friedrich Schelling (1775–1854) of 1809, for instance, identified God's existence as activity, and asserted that human activity is an expression of God's life: "God can only reveal himself in creatures who resemble him, in free, self-activating beings."[18]

It was against this intellectual milieu that the later Schleiermacher developed his Christological actualism. Actualism is a broad philosophical way of understanding being in terms of act. Schleiermacher claims that we can know Christ as God incarnate only insofar as Christ is understood as the pure activity of God's love, rather than the immutable God who became human without ceasing to be God.[19] In this way, theology as the study of history is for Schleiermacher a mediation between scientific inquiry and metaphysical knowledge of God's being-as-act.

Despite his deeply metaphysical intentions, then, the ultimate cost of Schleiermacher's theological turn to history in subsequent developments through the nineteenth century was that theology became an increasingly naturalistic enterprise. By the second half of the nineteenth century, the word *scientific* as a predicate for *theology* in the liberal tradition, broadly speaking, had basically come to mean that it is a positivist study of natural, historical phenomena, just like any other science. It was no longer a science composed of human knowledge of God qua God.

One dominant school in the broad liberal theological tradition of the nineteenth century was that of the Ritschlians. Albrecht Ritschl (1822–89) was a proponent of Hegelian philosophy in his early years, owing to the influence of his teacher, F. C.

18. F. W. J. Schelling, *Philosophical Inquiries into the Nature of Human Freedom*, trans. James Gutmann (Chicago: Open Court, 2003), 19.

19. See Kevin Hector, "Actualism and Incarnation: The High Christology of Friedrich Schleiermacher," *International Journal of Systematic Theology* 8, 3 (2006): 307–22.

Baur. In 1856, Ritschl publicly announced his break with Baur and the New Tübingen School. Staunchly opposed to what he perceived to be Hegel's metaphysical theology, Ritschl resorted to Kantian positivism in an effort to strip theology of every last vestige of metaphysical speculation.

Two important figures in the Ritschlian school who lived into the twentieth century were Wilhelm Herrmann (1846–1922) and Adolf von Harnack (1851–1930). Whereas the later Ritschl still saw history as God's purposive activity in some way, Herrmann and Harnack were more consistently "Kantian": they "moved beyond historicism" and no longer saw history as purposively progressing toward any consummate end point.[20]

Against this back-to-Kant movement that dominated much of neo-Protestant theology in the late nineteenth century, the works of Ernst Troeltsch (1865–1923) represented a last-ditch effort to revive the metaphysical historicism of post-Kantian idealism. The Reformed reader may be interested to learn that Troeltsch befriended Kuyper when their respective times in Heidelberg overlapped. Troeltsch was intrigued by Kuyper's exposition and application of historic Reformed theology. There are so many references to Kuyper in Troeltsch's famous *Social Teaching of the Christian Churches* that the latter refers to the former as a theologian "who has often been mentioned" in the book.[21]

The sharp eschatological consciousness in Kuyper's historicist worldview was for Troeltsch an example of how theological reflections on history can provide a basis on which all social life and human existence may strive toward God's final purpose for the world. Troeltsch's approach to history, however, is admittedly rooted in the idealist tradition of Schleiermacher, of

20. Zachhuber, "Historical Turn," 66.
21. Ernst Troeltsch, *The Social Teachings of the Christian Churches*, trans. Olive Wyon, 2 vols. (Louisville: WJK, 1992), 685.

which Kuyper is severely (though not without charity) critical.[22] Despite this difference, and despite Troeltsch's correct dismissal of Kuyper's shaky historical scholarship, the former could speak of the latter with overall approval and admiration, not least because they shared similar apologetic concerns in defending Christian theology against the onslaught of a broadly Kantian naturalism in the scientific arena. (Recall that Kant is not a naturalist or even deist with regard to special revelation, but he is a naturalist with regard to science.)

The beginning of the First World War marked the end of the so-called long nineteenth century. Established liberal theologians united themselves in support of German military actions, believing that the *Geist* of the German Eagle was finally about to soar and bring history to its divinely predetermined consummation. Upon witnessing such outright idolatry, a group of young theologians in the Teutonic parts of Europe declared the liberal tradition bankrupt. The back-to-Kant movement in modern theology—despite the idolatry of the neo-Kantians—became significant in an unprecedented way: Kant's Critical philosophy prophetically, as it were, declared to the learned that God is not to be identified with anything that is of this world—not even the German *Vaterland*.

The form of Kantianism that Herrmann and Harnack espoused was deeply ingrained in the early theology of their venerated pupil, Karl Barth (1886–1968), whose father, Johann Friedrich "Fritz" Barth, had been a student of another representative of the Ritschlian school, Julius Kaftan (1848–1926). With the language of God as "wholly Other," the early Barth resorted to Kant, among others, to launch a powerful attack on what he considered to be liberal theology. Although (as I have argued in my recent academic publications) it is problematic to interpret

22. See Zachhuber, "Historical Turn," 67.

the later Barth in a post-Kantian framework, and although he did break with his Ritschlian teachers both nominally and substantively, Kant's critique of metaphysics and its reception in liberal theology would continue to inform Barth's mature theology in significant ways.

Barth's dogmatics, as a whole, can be understood as a call for theology to be truly theological again: let scientific theology be the study of the self-revealed God, rather than the mere study of history, nature, social phenomena, culturally conditioned texts, etc. He succeeded to the extent of convincing a whole generation of theologians educated in the broad neo-Protestant tradition that theology can and must be the science of God.

Yet despite Barth's insistence that God is being-in-act, rather than being-as-act, Barth's Christocentrism is still so actualistic that he firmly rejected the possibility for theology to be a system of knowledge: we know God only as being-in-act, and as such, God cannot be pinned down in any system of human knowledge. This means that Barth also rejected the originally idealist notion of a Christian worldview, for *worldview* (*Weltanschauung*) and *system* (*System*) go hand in hand. At the end, even if Barth succeeded in qualifying theology as a science, the sense in which it is "scientific" cannot be fundamentally univocal with the sense in which, say, physics or sociology is scientific. This lack of univocity calls into question whether it is still meaningful to speak of theology as a *science*. Theology as such can no longer serve as the Queen of the Sciences, to guide us in thinking God's thoughts after him in all other branches of knowledge.

Kant on Divine Incomprehensibility and Revelation: A Reformed Assessment

Kant effectively banished theology from the realm of the sciences. Schleiermacher sought to restore the scientific status of theology by turning it into a historical science. Theology lost its distinct identity among the sciences. Barth attempted to reestablish theology as the study of God qua God, but the object of theological inquiries was, for him, so wholly other that theology was altogether separated from all the other sciences. The Kantian dilemma remains: theology qua theology is still in exile from the scientific realm.

Modern confessional Reformed theologians reacting to this Kantian problem showed a concerted attempt to reestablish theology as a science distinct yet inseparable from all the other sciences.[23] Bavinck's incisive response to Kant, in particular, hits the Achilles' heel. Bavinck recognizes that Kant's fundamental failure lies in the disjunction between general and special revelation on the ontic side, and knowledge and faith on the noetic side. We will discuss Bavinck's faith-seeking-understanding program in the next section.

Unlike Van Til, who interprets Kant as an empirical skeptic along Berkeleian and Humean lines, Bavinck's reading is much more balanced and charitable. He rightly points out that confessional Reformed theology is in agreement with Kant's limitation of human knowledge to the realm of experience. "Kant is perfectly correct when he says that our knowledge does not extend farther than our experience."[24]

Bavinck acknowledges that, regarding God's essential unknowability, Kant is at one with the official confessions of

---

23. Anglophone theologians such as Hodge used the word *science* to refer more specifically to the natural sciences. Thus, Hodge only metaphorically likened theology to science: "The Bible is to the theologian what nature is to the man of science." There is no question, however, that Hodge thought of theology as systematic knowledge of truths about God, which is the sense in which Kuyper and Bavinck spoke of theology as a science in the Continental context. See Charles Hodge, *Systematic Theology*, vol. 1 (Grand Rapids: Eerdmans, 1989), 10.

24. Herman Bavinck, *Reformed Dogmatics*, ed. John Bolt, trans. John Vriend, 4 vols. (Grand Rapids: Baker, 2003–8), 2:50.

both Catholicism and the Reformation. Latin orthodoxy, handed down from Augustine, Anselm, and Thomas to Luther and Calvin, teaches that the transcendent God is incomprehensible, that is, unknowable *per essentiam*. The tradition teaches that the finite is incapable of comprehending the infinite (*finitum non capax infiniti*). God became indirectly knowable to us only in and through his works, which are self-revelatory as he willed and wills them to be.

Well before Kant, reports Bavinck, Thomas Aquinas already taught that immediate knowledge of God is impossible within this world. "On earth the knowledge of God is mediate."[25] Even "faith-knowledge" given through "special revelation," per Thomas, "does not give us a knowledge of God *per essentiam* . . . . There is no [immediate] knowledge of God's essence, his 'whatness,' in terms of its uniqueness; we only know his disposition toward his creatures."[26] Catholic theology after the Reformation reaffirmed "scholasticism and again adopted the doctrine of the unknowability of God's essence in the way Thomas understood it," and "the Reformation did not modify this view."[27] Seventeenth-century Reformed orthodox theologians followed through with this view more relentlessly and consistently than Catholics and Lutherans. The Reformed "unanimously affirm that God infinitely surpasses our understanding, imagination, and language."[28]

In chapter 2, we saw that philosophy and theology in the eighteenth century had become optimistic about natural human reason's capacity to know God as God knows himself. "As the Reformation tradition's consciousness of divine incomprehensibility waned, philosophers, notably Kant, reaffirmed it."[29] As

---

25. Bavinck, *Reformed Dogmatics*, 2:39.
26. Bavinck, *Reformed Dogmatics*, 2:39.
27. Bavinck, *Reformed Dogmatics*, 2:40.
28. Bavinck, *Reformed Dogmatics*, 2:40–41.
29. Bavinck, *Reformed Dogmatics*, 2:28.

Bavinck sees it, Kant's critique of human reason, taken on its own, is nothing new or foreign to mainstream Latin Christianity.

On this particular point, Bavinck's assessment of Kant has been confirmed in recent times with the rigor of contemporary scholarship. Professor John Hare has shown that Kant's Critical philosophy and pure religion consistently avoid presupposing special revelation and remain within the bounds of general revelation and natural reason. Kant's assertion that the contents of special revelation are "unintelligible" to human beings "within the domain of reason" is perfectly in agreement with confessional Reformed theology.[30] "There should be nothing scandalous in the project of seeing how much of the gospel is intelligible in terms of general revelation."[31]

In this light, I should point out, from a Reformed perspective, that Kant's separation of philosophy from the domain of special revelation is not entirely foreign to the Reformation. This separation is well in line with the spirit of Luther's 1518 Heidelberg Disputation. Kant was a philosopher. He was also a Christian. From a Lutheran perspective, these two identities rightly belong to two different domains. Philosophy pertains to natural reason, which Kant had to critique in order to leave room for the domain of faith.

Professor Hare points out, contra popular opinion among Christians as well as secularists, that "Kant is not a deist about special revelation."[32] Among "Christians who know about Kant," he is often "lumped into 'the Enlightenment' without remainder."[33] Bavinck, too, errs in this respect. He thinks that "Kant is still situated completely in the eighteenth century."[34] It is true that

30. Hare, *Moral Gap*, 33.
31. Hare, *Moral Gap*, 35.
32. Hare, *Moral Gap*, 38.
33. Hare, *Moral Gap*, 35.
34. Bavinck, *Reformed Dogmatics*, 1:164.

Kant considers himself a "pure rationalist" with regard to revelation, but Bavinck is mistaken in thinking that being "purely rationalistic" is to hold that "the historical and positive has no value."[35]

There are in fact ample evidences for us to be "convinced that he [Kant] personally continued to believe in the central doctrines he was brought up with."[36] The theory that his employment of ecclesial rhetoric and frequent use of biblical references were meant to tailor to the religiosity of the general public and government officials does not stand in light of the evidences we now have.[37] More importantly, as we saw in chapter 2, Kant even reserved a place for special revelation in his philosophy: pure religion is unattainable for naked human reason, unless it is cloaked with historical faith. Bavinck is thus wrong to say that historical and positive revelation have "no value" to Kant's pure rationalism.

Yet the fact remains that Kant is "silent about his personal religious beliefs" in his philosophical writings.[38] This telling fact reflects how "the pure rationalist accepts special revelation but nevertheless does not think its acceptance is without qualification necessary to [pure] religion."[39] Faith and special revelation, as we saw in chapter 2, are necessary to the rational religion of the philosopher only in practice, but not in theory. It is in practice very difficult to make restaurant-quality sugar crust on a crème brûlée without a torch, though in theory an oven can also do the trick. For those who are not adept at using ovens, the torch is indeed necessary. Yet sugar is the *sine qua non* of the crust; the torch is not. Similarly, natural reason and general revelation are the indispensable ingredients for the philosopher's pure religion, while special revelation is only a necessary vehicle to emulate

35. Bavinck, *Reformed Dogmatics*, 1:164.
36. Hare, *Moral Gap*, 38.
37. See Palmquist, "Introduction," in Kant, *Religion*, xv–xvii.
38. Hare, *Moral Gap*, 38.
39. Hare, *Moral Gap*, 44–45.

pure religion. While Kant "accepts special revelation," he "holds that it is not a necessary requisite for pure religion."[40] Christianity can, in theory, be replaced with any other religion that does the same job. Kant knew very little about Islam, but it is fair to say that Judaism is, for him, like the oven that can be used in the absence of a torch.

So we should grant that Kant was not a deist or the kind of rationalist that Bavinck thought he was. Kant was at once a Christian and a philosopher. Because Christianity plays such an important role in his philosophy, he might even be considered a Christian philosopher of some sort. His understanding of faith and natural reason may well be in line with Lutheran doctrine, and so he is not as far away from Christianity as most Christians and secularists are accustomed to think.

But Kant certainly was not a Christian philosopher in a Reformed sense. A Christian philosopher, from the viewpoint of the basic Reformed understanding of faith and reason, is one who presupposes faith and special revelation in using reason to make sense of general revelation. I will contend, from this Reformed perspective, that Kant's attempt to make sense of the natural and moral world ultimately fails. How and why it fails is what we will discuss in the next two sections, where we will also provide Reformed solutions to Kant's problems.

Faith Seeking Understanding:
A Reformed-Anselmian Response to Kant

As suggested earlier, Bavinck's response to Kant highlights the very quintessence of the Reformed understanding of faith and knowledge in relation to special and general revelation. This does not mean that Bavinck is entirely correct in his interpretation of

40. Hare, *Moral Gap*, 42.

Kant. The errors pointed out above point to a more fundamental mistake in Bavinck's reading: he labels Kant as an agnostic who denies not only God's comprehensibility *per essentiam* (which traditional Christianity also denies), but also God's knowability in and through revelation. This description of Kant is based not on any textual evidence, but merely on a slippery-slope or strawman inference on Bavinck's part.[41]

The fact, as we have seen, is that Kant not only presupposes general revelation as a necessary condition for natural reason to make sense of reality, but also reserves a place for special revelation in his moral philosophy. When he says that the transcendental ideas—God, freedom, and immortality—become immanent and constitutive in the practical use of reason, he means that we do possess some form of knowledge of God. This knowledge is practical, rather than theoretical: we know that we ought to affirm that God is, but we do not know whether, in fact, God is. What Kant denies is scientific knowledge of God, for science is, by his definitions, theoretical, rather than practical. In fact, Bavinck acknowledges this about Kant as well.[42]

Overall, then, Bavinck is still right about Kant: the biblical proclamation, *God is*, pertains to the realm of faith, rather than knowledge. We know that *God ought to be*, but we can only believe that *God is*. Bavinck refers to Kant's distinctions between opinion, faith, and knowledge. According to Kant, "'thinking' [opinion] was to hold a thing to be true on insufficient grounds, 'believing' on subjectively sufficient grounds, and 'knowing' on objectively sufficient grounds."[43]

Bavinck in fact agrees with these basic distinctions, for they are rooted in Latin Christianity. He cites Augustine, Thomas, Zanchius, and Bonaventure to explain the intricacies of the

41. Bavinck, *Reformed Dogmatics*, 2:50.
42. Bavinck, *Reformed Dogmatics*, 2:42.
43. Bavinck, *Reformed Dogmatics*, 1:577.

opinion-faith-knowledge distinctions. In Augustine, the distinctions are between opinion, faith, and understanding; in Thomas and Zanchius, between opinion, faith, and science; and in Bonaventure, faith as "certainty of assent" and science as "certainty of speculation."[44]

In saying that the distinctions are "more correctly defined" by the Latin theologians, Bavinck appears to be hinting at the most fundamental difference between Kant and traditional Christianity. In the faith-seeking-understanding tradition, faith is the beginning of knowledge. Faith and understanding are not two different forms, but rather two stages of knowledge. The Christian knows God by faith and seeks to attain systematic understanding of God. Theology as a science, then, begins with faith in the self-revealed God.

In Kant, by contrast, faith does not qualify as knowledge. Faith does not even pertain to the practical knowledge of rational religion. Of the two concentric circles of rational religion and revealed religion, biblical faith is at home in the latter and only peripheral to the former (see chapter 2). Bavinck rightly comments that in Kant's

> critical examination of the human faculty of cognition this philosopher came to the conclusion that the supernatural is unattainable for us human beings . . . . But next to this form of knowing there is room for a faith that . . . postulates the existence of God, and the soul and its immortality. However, these postulates are not scientific theses capable of rigorous proof. . . . Accordingly, believing and knowing are *separated* in principle, each having its own domain. In the sensuous world, science is possible; with respect to the super-sensuous, we have to be satisfied with faith.[45]

44. Bavinck, *Reformed Dogmatics*, 1:577–78.
45. Bavinck, *Reformed Dogmatics*, 1:35 (italics added).

It is precisely this Kantian separation of faith and knowledge into two different domains that Bavinck finds problematic.

The truth is that all systematic claims to knowledge must, explicitly or not, begin with faith in something. Cartesian rationalism admittedly subscribes to a faith-seeking-understanding program. This faith is in the existence and permanence of the rational self, the *ego cogito*. Empiricists from Locke to Hume believed in the reality of that which is perceived, and this, as we have seen, was implicitly an extension of Cartesian faith in the ideas of the mind.

In rejecting the Enlightenment mode of the faith-seeking-understanding project, Kant gave rise to a distinctively modern prejudice against faith. For him, there is room for faith only outside the domain of knowledge. Yet he is at odds with himself here, because even his transcendental idealism begins with faith in something.

In chapter 2, we offered a charitable reading of Kant that takes him to be the empirical realist that he claims to be. To understand him as such, we adopted what Karl Ameriks calls a "regressive approach" in interpreting Kant's transcendental idealism. This means that

> the proper way to begin to understand Kant's views . . . is to recognize that . . . he always starts from, and holds to, the fact that there is a real interaction of finite substances. . . . He proceeds from what he takes to be a common ground on which this hypothesis is irrelevant: we are finite beings always believing that we are affected by at least some other finite beings, and we recognize that other personal beings also hold that.[46]

46. Karl Ameriks, *Interpreting Kant's* Critiques (Oxford: Oxford University Press, 2003), 25.

Ameriks contends that this "common ground" that Kant presupposes is not "a matter of 'faith,'" but here Ameriks is speaking of "faith" in the sense of "something that we make an effort to hold onto or that requires a special intuitive faculty or complex speculative or emotional attitude."[47] According to Kant's own definitions, however, faith is an ordinary act of the intellect. Kant's transcendental idealism, if understood regressively, obviously proceeds from faith (as understood in accordance with Kant's own definition) in the reality of external objects and their interactions.

Of course, faith in the reality of the objects of experiences fundamentally differs from faith in God's existence. That we possess knowledge of the world of experience is for Kant a basic fact that we can take for granted. God, however, is beyond experience. If we can claim to have knowledge of God, such knowledge can only be purely speculative. The question is, can speculative reason attain unto knowledge of God?

As we saw in chapter 2, Kant points out that among all the arguments for God's existence in traditional metaphysics, only the ontological proof is purely speculative. He thinks that if the putative knowledge of God rendered by the ontological argument is an illusion, then it can be settled once and for all that theoretical knowledge of God's existence is impossible, and that theology can never be scientific.

We then saw how Kant dismantles Descartes's ontological argument. It is important to note—and many Kant scholars have missed this—that Kant's refutation is explicitly directed at the *Cartesian* formulation of the argument, "the famous ontological (Cartesian) proof of a highest being from concepts."[48] This is rather curious, because the best-known representative of this

---

47. Ameriks, *Interpreting Kant's* Critiques, 25.
48. Kant, *Critique of Pure Reason*, A602/B630.

family of theistic proofs is Anselm, not Descartes. Although there is no clear textual indication whether Kant thinks his refutation also applies to the Anselmian formulation, there are at least two reasons why I think Kant intends to restrict his arguments to the Cartesian version.

First, in the section titled "on the impossibility of an ontological proof of God's existence," Anselm's name is not mentioned at all.[49] Is this because Kant is unfamiliar with Anselm or because, for some reason, Kant does not intend to address the Anselmian formulation of the proof? Given the fact that Kant matriculated as a theology student at the University of Königsberg, there is little reason to suppose that he was not equipped to deal with Anselm.

Second, the section on the ontological proof pertains to Kant's discussion of "transcendental illusions," under the rubric of "transcendental dialectic," which treats "pure reason as the seat of transcendental illusion."[50] Anselm's revealed theology does not pertain to pure reason; Descartes's transcendental theology does. Anselm's proof is not concerned with the abstract existence of the god of rational theology. Rather, he presupposes the concretely triune existence of the God self-revealed in Scripture.

Kant is very specific that his Critical philosophy is aimed at critiquing rational philosophy, rather than faith in revealed theology. Some have argued that Kant's avoidance of revealed theology in his writings had to do with political censorship at the time, but we saw in chapter 2 that this avoidance is in fact consistent with his Critical philosophy as a whole. It thus seems reasonable to hold that Anselm's towering figure is completely out of sight in the section on the ontological proof, precisely because Kant intends for his refutation to be directed specifically at the Cartesian model, not the Anselmian.

49. Kant, *Critique of Pure Reason*, A592/B620–A602/B630.
50. Kant, *Critique of Pure Reason*, A298/B354.

At this juncture, we must note that Descartes and Anselm differ fundamentally in their respective starting points. The formal resemblance is, of course, obvious—so much so that later scholars who do not recognize the fundamental difference between the two have commented that speculative philosophers in the Cartesian tradition, notably Hegel, echo "Anselm's *credo ut intelligam* faith" as "the foundation for speculative philosophizing."[51]

Anselm's faith, however, is in the triune Creator, whose perfections are made known to us through revelation: his definitions of God's perfections are strictly delimited in biblical terms. Although Anselm's treatment of the Trinity in *Proslogion* is brief, latent in it is a powerful answer to Kant. Recall that for Kant, determinacy is a criterion of knowledge. Something is determinate only when its being is affirmed or negated on the ground of an other. If God is indeed the only true ideal of pure reason—an idea of the highest rank—then it can never satisfy the criterion of determinacy, for there is no idea of equal rank against which God can be determinately compared. For the abstract idea of a supreme being such as that found in Descartes's ontological argument, then, there can never be any determinate knowledge of its existence.

In orthodox Trinitarian doctrine, however, God is not an abstract ideal. God exists concretely as Father, Son, and Holy Spirit, each possessing the fullness of God's being.[52] Anselm, following Augustine, speaks of the Trinity in terms of love. Love is an act that requires an object. But because God is triune, he needs no object outside himself in order to *be* love. The triune God *is* love: he is at once the lover, the beloved, and the act of love. He does not *become* love upon the condition of an other outside

51. Howard Kainz, "Hegel, Providence, and the Philosophy of History," *Hegel-Jahrbuch* (1995): 184.

52. Anselm of Canterbury, *Proslogium*, in *St. Anselm: Basic Writings* (Chicago: Open Court, 1962), 74–75.

his being. God *is*, and his *being* is determinate in and for himself (*an und für sich*—if I may be excused for a little "Hegeling"). He needs no other outside himself in order to become determinate as God. Knowledge of the triune God, then, already meets the criterion of determinacy at the initial stage of faith. It is from faith in the triune Creator that Anselm proceeds with his "proof."

In other words, we can be endowed with determinate knowledge of God because God has revealed himself in relation to himself in the persons of the Trinity. Already latent in Anselm's argument is the historical nature of this revelation. It is through redemptive history (creation-fall-redemption), centering on the person and work of Christ, that God supremely reveals himself and his will to us. In the Gospels, we see concrete interactions between the Father, the Son, and the Holy Spirit in the person of Jesus Christ. God comes into relationship with the creature without ceasing to *be* God, because his immutable essence is already relational in and for itself.

The rationalist gulf between the contingent truths of history and necessary truths of reason is overcome only if we presuppose the self-revelation of the immutably triune God in and through history. In and through the history of redemption, the eternal *being* of God is truly revealed to us, without being reduced to the process of *becoming*.

It is true that theologians of the neo-Calvinist heritage are generally dismissive of Anselm's ontological argument. Bavinck, for instance, opines that Anselm's "scholastic speculation" operates on a "naïve confidence that faith could be elevated to the level of knowledge."[53] Yet his understanding of the form of the argument presented in Anselm's *Proslogion* is problematic. Bavinck thinks that the proof "proceeds from the necessity of thinking the highest absolute idea, that is, of the idea of God, and concludes

53. Bavinck, *Reformed Dogmatics*, 1:146.

from it the actual existence of that idea, since otherwise it would not be the absolute or greatest idea."[54] Though he recognizes distinctions between the Cartesian and the Anselmian forms of the proof, he sometimes slips into a confusion of the two and speaks of "the form given to it by Anselm and Descartes."[55]

What Bavinck misses here is that Anselm's demonstration is reductive, rather than deductive. That is, Anselm does not deduce God's existence from the necessity of thinking the idea of God. His starting point is God's concrete triune existence as revealed in Scripture and, in the form of a *reductio ad absurdum*, argues that if we did not presuppose the God of Scripture, our thoughts and ideas would not be able to avoid irrationality and contradictions. Thus, Anselm calls both his *Monologion* and *Proslogion* "an example of meditation on the grounds of faith."[56]

In the form of a prayer, Anselm says that his purpose is "to understand that thou art as we believe; and that thou art that which we believe."[57] The belief is this: "we believe that thou art a being than which nothing greater can be conceived."[58] To Anselm, however, the veracity of our belief in the existence of the perfect being greater than which nothing can be conceived is not deductively possible. Although even the fool is endowed with the idea of the perfect being, what "we believe" regarding God has to be given to us through special revelation.

In *Proslogion*, chapter 4, Anselm argues that an abstract philosophical idea of God can reasonably be conceived as nonexistent. Only the concrete God of Scripture is the perfect being whom we cannot rationally conceive to be nonexistent.[59] Thus,

54. Bavinck, *Reformed Dogmatics*, 1:84.
55. Bavinck, *Reformed Dogmatics*, 1:79.
56. Anselm, *Proslogium*, 47.
57. Anselm, *Proslogium*, 53.
58. Anselm, *Proslogium*, 53.
59. Anselm, *Proslogium*, 55–56.

in the ensuing chapters, Anselm proceeds to outline the concrete perfections of God in biblical terms. He begins, in Augustinian fashion, with God's transcendence in terms of *creatio ex nihilo* (chapter 5).[60] Then he delineates God's attributes and perfections in biblical terms (chapters 6–13).[61] He defines God's infinity as being "uncircumscribed and eternal" (chapter 14), and returns to this notion with the concrete delimitation that "thou art, outside all time. For yesterday and to-day and to-morrow have no existence, except in time; but thou, although nothing exists without thee, nevertheless dost not exist in space or time" (chapter 19).[62] God's eternality is then defined in terms of timelessness and simultaneity (chapters 20–21).[63] This also entails God's simplicity (chapter 18).[64] Indeed, God is self-existent: "Therefore, thou alone, O Lord, art what thou art; and thou art he who thou art" (chapter 22).[65] God is self-existent as the perfect being as such, not as an abstract idea, but only in his concrete triune existence (chapter 23).[66]

A crucial point that sets Anselm apart from Descartes is chapter 15: "Therefore, O Lord, thou art not only that than which a greater cannot be conceived, but thou art a being greater than can be conceived."[67] This is a proclamation of God's unknowability *per essentiam*, right in the middle of statements of what we know about God in and through special revelation. Cartesian speculation assumes that human reason can attain some God's-eye view of God himself. The Cartesian god is comprehensible; its immanence is affirmed at the expense of

60. Anselm, *Proslogium*, 56–57.
61. Anselm, *Proslogium*, 57–66.
62. Anselm, *Proslogium*, 67, 71.
63. Anselm, *Proslogium*, 72–73.
64. Anselm, *Proslogium*, 69–71.
65. Anselm, *Proslogium*, 73.
66. Anselm, *Proslogium*, 74–75.
67. Anselm, *Proslogium*, 68.

transcendence. Conceptually, then, this god is really no God at all. But because Anselm's God is the incomprehensible God revealed to us in Scripture, Anselm knows better than Descartes. Anselm knows that God is greater than can be conceived by human speculation. Therefore, he has to start with faith in special revelation in order to seek understanding of how we have already known God to be the God that *is*.

In other words, Anselm presupposes that the Christian already knows God by faith, and he wants to understand how this was ontologically possible. Professor John Frame thus rightly portrays Anselm as a proto-presuppositional thinker who presented his argument "in a prayer of profound Christian devotion" and stood firm on the conviction that "the ontological argument proves the biblical God only if it presupposes distinctively Christian values and a Christian view [of God's perfections]."[68]

Descartes's faith, diametrically opposed to that of Anselm, is in the rationality of the thinking *ego*. The self-revelation of the triune Creator greater than whom nothing can exist is, for Anselm, the only ground on which I can rationally reflect on God's existence: *God is*, therefore *I think* (upon the premise of special revelation). Descartes's revolutionary mind overturns this order. For Descartes, my indubitable rationality is that which guarantees to me the existence of God: *I think*, therefore *God is*.

The existence of God as a perfect being, according to Descartes, provides rational certainty for the justification of my belief that the world external to my mind is real. The thrust of the argument is that God, who created the world, endowed me with sensory organs and that because as a perfect being he is, of conceptual necessity, omnibenevolent and truthful, I can trust that the world that I perceive with my senses is real. In

---

68. John M. Frame, *Apologetics: A Justification of Christian Belief* (Phillipsburg, NJ: P&R Publishing, 2015), 120–22.

other words, I know in the first instance, in the immediacy of faith, that I exist as a rational being. My rationality then mediates between this faith and the understanding that God and the world are real.

What is excluded in this revolutionary version of the faith-seeking-understanding program is revelation as the work of God that mediates between the very truth of God and our knowledge of this truth. And herein lies the very essence of early-modern rationalism, which Kant discloses to us in his first *Critique*: its basis is faith in human rationality, and it constitutes a speculative attempt to grasp the metaphysical truths and substance of the whole of reality apart from divine revelation. Kant is right that ontological proof of an abstract god of philosophy is doomed to fail. Anselm's God, however, is the concrete God of Scripture. His intellectual knowledge of God's existence is determinate and concrete.

God, History, and Science: A Neo-Calvinist Understanding

There is no reason, as far as I can see, for Reformed Christians to disagree with Kant's demonstration of the failure of Cartesian faith. Kant's own failure, from a Christian point of view, will be directly proportional to the extent to which one takes his position as a refusal to adopt an Anselmian mode of the faith-seeking-understanding program. Anselmian faith is faith in the God of special revelation, and so, for Kant, it plays no constitutive role in scientific knowledge. Scientific knowledge requires determinacy, but the abstract idea of God as the ideal of pure reason is, by conceptual definition, undeterminable. For the purpose of science, we must exercise faith in the reality and order of the natural and moral world, but faith in the Creator of this world has only a regulative place in the sciences. Kant is right that scientific knowledge requires determinacy, but as demonstrated earlier, Anselmian knowledge of the triune Creator is concrete and determinate from the very beginning of the faith-seeking-understanding program. Refusal to adopt this mode of thinking is a fundamental cause of Kant's failure.

But what is Kant's failure, anyway? Recall that his critique of reason was partly aimed at securing the sciences from the threats of Humean skepticism. The banishment of theology from the sciences, however, meant that there was no longer an academic discipline to lend cohesion to our knowledge of this diverse world. It is a known fact that Kant had given up on the Wolffian attempt to search for systematic unity of the sciences. Wolff's Cartesian faith meant that there was still an abstract idea—the god of philosophy—that held the diverse sciences together. Scientific inquiries after Kant, however, increasingly broke up the sum of human knowledge into bits and pieces.

Part and parcel of the fragmentation of scientific knowledge is its naturalization. In the generation of Hegel, Schelling, and Schleiermacher, science in Continental Europe had become overwhelmingly naturalistic under the influence of Kant's Critical philosophy. Under Kant's influence, Bavinck observes, "the doctrine of the unknowability of God has progressively penetrated modern consciousness."[69] As a result, the modern sciences up to Bavinck's (and our own) day had been an increasingly naturalistic enterprise that attempted to strip itself of every last vestige of theistic understandings of divine providence—the "hand of God," so to say. Think, for example, of how Lagrangian and Hamiltonian mechanics came to dismiss even the Newtonian understanding of force, defined by the equation $F = ma$, as a "hand of God" or "God of the gaps" concept that is empirically unobserved and mathematically redundant.

69. Bavinck, *Reformed Dogmatics*, 2:43.

Bavinck's response to Kant is partly inspired by Hegel. Hegel, according to Bavinck, represents a hiatus in this historical progression of naturalistic consciousness in modern Europe.[70] Hegel attempted to offer a theistic understanding of science by reviving the faith-seeking-understanding mode of speculation handed down from Descartes. Philosophy, especially logic, is for Hegel the *concept* (*Begriff*) of science, that is, science in its pure form. As "the pure science" in which all sciences culminate, philosophy (especially logic) "is the description of God's being as such," that is, as "the Idea itself."[71] Scientific inquiry is for Hegel, as rightly understood by Bavinck, the process through which "Reason . . . raises itself step by step through several stages to the level of absolute knowledge, then looks at truth face to face and knows its essence to be Reason, Thought, the Idea itself."[72]

This theistic impulse of Hegel's speculative approach to science is precisely what Bavinck finds especially appealing and dangerous at the same time. Bavinck comments that when "supernaturalism succumbed under the blows of Rousseau and Kant, Lessing and Schleiermacher," it was Hegel who brought about "a mighty reversal."[73] It is in the theistic, rather than physical, "evolution" of the universe "that religion," especially its representation of divine providence, "had its place."[74]

Hegel's speculative approach to science, however, leads to results that contradict his own theistic intentions. First, Bavinck comments, "the crucial question" with regard to rationalism in general "is this: Do we think a thing because it exists or does a thing exist because we necessarily and logically have to think it?

---

70. Bavinck, *Reformed Dogmatics*, 2:43.
71. Hegel, *Science of Logic*, 10.
72. Bavinck, *Reformed Dogmatics*, 2:43.
73. Bavinck, *Reformed Dogmatics*, 1:517.
74. Bavinck, *Reformed Dogmatics*, 1:517.

Speculative philosophy affirmed the latter."[75] "But"—and herein lies Bavinck's criticism of Hegel's basically Cartesian mode of speculation—

> however much resemblance there may be between thought and existence, the difference between them is no less real. From thought one cannot conclude to existence because the existence of all creatures is not an emanation of thought but arises from an act of power. The essence of things is due to the thought of God; only their existence is due to his will. Human thought, accordingly, presupposes existence. It arises only upon the basis of the created world.[76]

Here Bavinck appears to be reiterating Kant's critique of Cartesian speculation: *cogito, ergo sum* is an analytical judgment, a judgment of clarification, rather than a proper inference, because "I think" already presupposes "I am." Bavinck continues to emphasize that "we can only reflect (*re*-flect) on that which has been *pre*-conceived and comes to our consciousness through the world."[77] This re-flection on the basis of pre-conception is precisely the Anselmian mode of scientific inquiry.

Hegel's scientific speculation, by contrast, is Cartesian. Its problem is that "if . . . one rejects all matter that has come to us from without and adopts as one's starting point pure reason . . . , one retains nothing, or at most a principle so general, so devoid of content and vague that nothing—let alone the entire universe or all of Christian revelation and religion—can be deduced from it."[78] Thus, Bavinck comments that "Hegel's philosophy was . . . not as harmless as it originally seemed to be. It was the working

75. Bavinck, *Reformed Dogmatics*, 1:521.
76. Bavinck, *Reformed Dogmatics*, 1:521.
77. Bavinck, *Reformed Dogmatics*, 1:521 (italics original).
78. Bavinck, *Reformed Dogmatics*, 1:521.

out and application of Fichte's thesis that the ego posits the non-ego, that the subject creates the object."[79]

Bavinck points out that Hegel's presupposition of ultimate divine-human identity inevitably obliterates the latter's very theistic intentions. This "became clear," Bavinck observes, in the immediately ensuing generation of Ludwig Feuerbach (1804–72) and David Friedrich Strauss (1808–74), who both purported to be followers of Hegel.[80] Bavinck aptly observes that the two erstwhile Berlin students both took Hegel's position that "God and man are one" to its logical end, and "both Feuerbach and Strauss ended up in materialism: sensual nature is the only reality; human beings are what they eat."[81] That is, the panentheistic core of Hegel's idealism inevitably leads to a materialistic and naturalistic worldview in which divine providence is excluded. Bavinck's prophetic mind knew very well that such a worldview would eventually (as Western societies have witnessed by now) strip the scientific enterprise of the legitimacy to ascribe meaning and purpose to the physical and even moral world.

How Bavinck builds on Hegel's response to Kant and construes a Reformed worldview to counter Hegel's own challenges to traditional Christianity is a topic that I introduce in some detail in my previous volume in the present series.[82] Let me give a summary here, albeit under a different arrangement, so that we can come to appreciate how Bavinck capitalizes on an Anselmian mode of faith-seeking-understanding inquiry.

First, Bavinck agrees with Hegel that Kant's exclusion of the constitutive role of faith in God from the sciences is ultimately catastrophic to the scientific enterprise. Human knowledge of

---

79. Bavinck, *Reformed Dogmatics*, 1:521.

80. Bavinck, *Reformed Dogmatics*, 1:166.

81. Bavinck, *Reformed Dogmatics*, 1:256.

82. Shao Kai Tseng, *G. W. F. Hegel* (Phillipsburg, NJ: P&R Publishing, 2018), 72–77, 106–16.

the diverse world would be broken into bits and pieces without what Hegel and Van Til call a *concrete universal*. As suggested earlier, Bavinck, unlike Barth, does not rest satisfied in merely securing the scientific status of theology. Bavinck's critical interactions with Kant through Hegel carry an important aim: he wants to ascertain the possibility of science as a *worldview* based on our knowledge of God.

Theology is, on Bavinck's neo-Calvinist view, one of the many sciences. In this sense, theology is scientific in the same way that, say, sociology and physics are scientific, in that it makes constitutive claims about God in the theoretical use of reason. On the other hand, theology is unique among the sciences, for it is the only discipline of knowledge that accounts for an object that is ultimately actual and rational. Theology is, as such, the only science that regulates (i.e., lends unity to) the diverse sciences to enable a scientific worldview.

Worldview (German: *Weltanschauung*; Dutch: *wereldbeschouwing*) is perhaps better translated as "world intuition." It originated from German idealism. Kant rejected the thought that human beings may gain intellectual intuition of the world: only God knows the world immediately (see chapter 2). Our intellectual understanding can never be intuitive. When post-Kantian idealists invented the term *Weltanschauung*, they intended to argue that systematic human understandings of the world find their starting point in faith as an act of the intellect that intuits some object.

Kant's transcendental idealism was dubbed a "critique of immediacy," and figures such as Johann Gottlieb Fichte (1762–1814), the early Friedrich Schelling (1775–1854), and the early Schleiermacher resorted to various notions of immediacy or direct identity between the essence and act of the (self-)conscious *ego*, the divine and the human, the infinite and the finite, and what not, to contend for the possibility of intellectual world intuitions. By 1807—the year that *Phenomenology of Spirit* was published—Hegel had found this idealist philosophy of immediacy deeply troubling. He famously mocked the early Schelling's identity metaphysics as "the night in which . . . all cows are black."[83] Still, Hegel revived the Cartesian mode of faith-seeking-understanding speculation, in an attempt to establish the possibility of our *after-thinking* (*Nachdenken*) of the world and its history to lead to *reflection* (*Reflexion*) of the pure essence of reason, that is, God. In Hegel, then, faith is an act of the intellect that intuits the immediate actualities of the world in order to come to reflective, mediated, and comprehensive understandings of its developed actualities in light of the idea of God.

With one accord, Hegel and the other idealists of his generation insisted, against Kant, that only in light of some idea of God can particular phenomena in this world and its history be systematically understood. Hegel, in particular, pointed out that this idea cannot be merely an intuitive feeling (as Schleiermacher would have it). We must develop, on the basis of intuitive faith, scientific and theoretical explications of our idea of God, for otherwise, the diverse phenomena that we observe would lose their noetic unity. Theoretical knowledge would then be reduced to bits and pieces, and no scientific system would be possible, much less any scientific worldview.

Second, though Kant is not a deist or naturalist with regard to revelation, he is nevertheless a naturalist with regard to science. On his view, faith and supernatural revelation play only a regulative role in scientific knowledge. T. F. Torrance vividly describes this view of science as a "fatal deistic disjunction between God and the world."[84]

---

83. Georg Wilhelm Friedrich Hegel, *Phenomenology of Spirit*, ed. Terry Pinkard and Michael Baur, trans. Michael Baur (Cambridge: Cambridge University Press, 2018), 12.

84. Thomas F. Torrance, *Space, Time and Resurrection* (Edinburgh: T&T Clark, 1976), 2.

What this disjunction means, as Hegel and Bavinck rightly see it, is that scientific knowledge can no longer identify meaning and purpose in the physical and moral world. Yet teleology is so deeply embedded in our *a priori* category of causation that our sciences, no matter how naturalistic they have become, have never successfully eradicated the human impulse to identify progress and purpose behind immanent phenomena.

Our presentation of modern theology in the previous section in fact reflects a deeper contradiction symptomatic of post-Kantian modernity, namely, the contradiction between historicism and naturalistic positivism. On one hand, the historicist impulse to identify progress and development must presuppose some idea of supernatural intervention. On the other hand, positivism presupposes that nature is blind and purposeless. This contradiction does not undergird only the historical-critical scholarships of the New Tübingen and Ritschlian Schools or the historical objectivism of the celebrated historian Leopold von Ranke (1795–1886). The Darwinian refusal to see evolution as a blind process also reveals the inadequacy of Kant's naturalistic view of science: it cannot render satisfactory knowledge of the world, for our quest for knowledge is never satisfied without its teleological dimension (a dimension that Kant in fact tries to retain, notwithstanding his naturalism).

Against Kant, the neo-Calvinist masters generally agreed with Hegel that scientific knowledge must be grounded in the theoretical knowledge of God. For Hegel, this knowledge must include not only God's creation of the world. The rationality of the world hinges on God's providential guidance of the world and its history. A world envisioned with mere natural order but without providential guidance is, per Hegel, like a machine that functions without ever being able to understand its purpose. The divorce between faith and knowledge that easily results from Kantian naturalism necessarily leads to such a mechanical view of the world. Hegel envisions the world organically: it is like a living organism that grows toward the end of its consummation under God's providential care.

In sharp contrast to neo-Calvinism, however, Hegel's idealism constitutes an attempt to revive the Cartesian mode of speculation once "extirpated root and branch" by Kant's critique of reason.[85] Hegelian speculation finds its basis in a presuppositional kind of faith in the *cogito* and the *sum* of human consciousness. Human reason necessitates God's existence and providence. Consequently, the Hegelian system, and idealism after it, reduces God to a rational concept. This is precisely why Bavinck so vehemently rejected the kind of speculative thinking culminating in Hegel.

According to historic Christianity, it is God's immutable triune existence and his works of creation and providence as an *ad extra* revelation of his essence that guarantees the rational structure of the human creature made in his image. God's existence is not dependent on human reason. Rather, God's being and works ground the rational structure of the created universe, as well as the possibility of the rationality of human knowledge of creation.

Bavinck is in agreement with Hegel that the concept of divine providence is a *sine qua non* for warranting the rationality of scientific reflections on the world and its history. Against Kant, Hegel was deeply wary that the increasingly naturalistic worldviews undergirding the various scientific disciplines of his day would inevitably strip away rationality from human understandings of the world. Hegel thus insisted on seeing the universe and its history as the outworking of an ultimately rational divine plan. Hegel's speculative starting point in human consciousness, however, means that he must posit a consummate divine-human

85. Hegel, *Science of Logic*, 7–8.

identity in order to uphold a providential view of the world. Providence, per Hegel, is not an *ad extra* outworking of God's will, but rather an evolution of God's very being-in-becoming. This amounts to a dissolution between primary (divine) and secondary (creaturely) causes, and thus a denial of the *concursus Dei*, the traditional doctrine that all events in creation are totally caused by God's actions on the one hand, and totally caused by the natural and moral order of creation on the other. Hegel's system leaves no room for any genuine concurrence of the primary cause with secondary causes.

In the Reformed doctrine of providence—especially that espoused by historic Dutch Calvinism—strong emphasis is placed on the divine *concursus* as the fundamental principle underlying the other two traditional principles, namely, divine *conservatio* ("conservation") and *gubernatio* ("ruling"). Louis Berkhof aptly observes that "Dutch dogmaticians" from the early-modern period on have given "the element of concurrence greater prominence, in order to guard against the dangers of both Deism and Pantheism."[86] The doctrine of *concursus Dei* guards the Christian worldview from Kant on the one hand and Hegel on the other.

Bavinck's formulation of the *concursus* maintains against Hegelian panentheism a strict Creator-creature distinction, as well as an abiding distinction in the inseparable union between God's being and works. God decided to create the universe by an *ad extra* act of his will that perfectly corresponds to his essence, but this act of the divine will is not, has never been, and will never be a necessary aspect of God's being. In other words, God did not, does not, and will never need the world as an other in order to actualize himself as God. Providence is the *ad extra* execution of God's will as a revelation of God's immutable essence.

---

86. Louis Berkhof, *Systematic Theology* (Edinburgh: Banner of Truth, 1958), 133.

It is not identical with God's essence, and it does not alter God's being in historical process.

Against Kant's prohibition of faith in scientific undertakings, neo-Calvinists such as Bavinck envision, with Hegel, providence in organic trinitarian patterns, in order to make sense of this world. The anthropocentric starting point of Hegel's speculative logic, however, means that his logical trinity, conceived in human image, is one in which God's being is ultimately dissolved in the moment of becoming. Hegel's organic metaphors are aimed at explicating the view that the Logic is a subject or living substance undergoing organic growth. The masters of neo-Calvinism concertedly argue that Hegel's logical-trinitarian organicism inevitably reduces the will of God to the common fate of humanity, destroying the boundaries between diverse natures within creation because of the ultimate (though not immediate) dissolution of the Creator-creature distinction.

The starting point of the science of theology, per neo-Calvinism and historic Reformed theology, is faith in the self-revealed triune God, whose absolute subjectivity is immutable. God is perfectly God in his triune essence qua Father, Son, and Holy Spirit. Creation and providence reveal God's essence but do not actualize, constitute, or determine it. But because God is the living God, in the Creator-creature relation-in-distinction, creation as the ectype is endowed with organic natures reflective of its immutable archetype in the pattern of unity and diversity.

Creation as a living entity, moreover, does not "grow" by itself. To borrow a famous expression from Karl Barth, creation and providential history are the "outward basis" of God's ideas, while the latter constitute the "inward basis" of the former. These ideas do not evolve into existence. Rather, they give rise to creaturely existence external to God's being via the act of *creatio ex nihilo*, and continue to sustain creaturely existences and progress in such a way that creation and its history—including the human mind!—are inherently revelational but not inherently divine (i.e., creatures are never emanations of divine natures or ideas). Van Til puts it splendidly: "taking the creation doctrine seriously involves thinking of man in his whole constitutional makeup as himself revelational of God. . . . Being itself revelational, the mind of man is made for the reception of revelation."[87]

Van Til's statement constitutes a powerful response to both Kant and Hegel. The Kantian view of *a priori* concepts rules out the possibility of theoretical knowledge of God's existence, and easily leads to a denial of the teleological dimension of human sciences that Kant in fact tries to retain throughout his writings. We are left with this science and that science, without a scientific worldview. The Hegelian view of providence, along with its faith-seeking-understanding speculation, restores this teleological dimension, but unavoidably leads to the dissolution of creaturely particularities in the grand uniformity of the God concept. We are left with a scientific worldview in which this science and that science are ultimately consumed by the unifying science of logic.

Neo-Calvinism, as a whole, constitutes an attempt to safeguard the diversity and unity of all forms of human knowledge. In that vein, Van Til stresses, with Kant, that our knowledge hinges on *a priori* concepts in the mind. With Hegel, Van Til also insists that God's immanent activity is necessary to sustain the systematic unity of human knowledge and retain its teleological dimension. "If human reason in all of its manipulations is itself in the first place wholly dependent upon a prior revelational activity of God and upon a constant, sustained revelational activity of God, then a supernatural revelational activity will not come to it as something strange."[88] This means, contra Kant, that

87. Cornelius Van Til, *An Introduction to Systematic Theology* (Phillipsburg, NJ: P&R Publishing, 2007), 266.

88. Van Til, *Introduction to Systematic Theology*, 266.

supernatural revelation is not adjacent to nature and reason without overlap and, contra Hegel, that nature and reason are only God's *ad extra* works of revelation that are in no way identical with God's essential being.

The inherently revelational nature of creation and history means that human understandings of the world can be rational, as long as we think God's thoughts after God. With Kant, and contra Descartes and Hegel, the Christian—especially the Reformed—insists that the human mind is not consummately rational. That is, we are not rational by absolute essentiality. Against Kant, however, the Christian insists that the rationality of scientific knowledge hinges on God's *ad extra* revelation—both general and special—and the divine gift of faith through regeneration. Only on the basis of faith in revelation as the beginning of constitutive knowledge of God in the theoretical use of reason can scientific and systematic attempts to understand the self, the world, and God affirm the rationality of human knowledge and its objects.

Van Til, despite his problematic interpretations, is right in pinpointing the definitive Reformed answer to Kant and post-Kantian modernity. Addressing the "modern man, brought up on the phenomenal-noumenal distinction of Immanuel Kant," Van Til proclaims that systematic human knowledge of the self, the world, and God must begin with the confession of faith, which admits of no other proof—empirical or transcendental—than its own truth stated in Scripture:

> There is but one only living and true God, who is infinite in being and perfection, a most pure spirit invisible, without body, parts, or passions, immutable, immense, eternal, incomprehensible, almighty, most wise, most holy, most free, most absolute, working all things according to the counsel of his own immutable and most righteous will, for his own glory; most

loving, gracious, merciful, long suffering, abundant in goodness and truth, forgiving iniquity, transgression, and sin, the rewarder of them that diligently seek him; and withal most just and terrible in his judgments; hating all sin, and who will by no means clear the guilty.[89]

Conclusion: Knowledge of God in Christ

"Now faith is the assurance of things hoped for, the conviction of things not seen. For by it the people of old received their commendation" (Heb. 11:1–2). The author of Hebrews tells us that it is "by faith" that "we understand" God's creation of the world by his word (v. 3). He then shows us that the faith by which we understand the world and its history—the faith for which the saints of old were commended—is a redemptive-historical faith centered on none other than the person and work of Jesus Christ. The "cloud of witnesses" named in Hebrews 11, with one accord, call us to fix our eyes on "Jesus, the founder and perfecter of our faith" (12:1–2).

For all who call on our Father in heaven, no knowledge is dearer to our hearts and closer to our minds than that of the triune God and what he has done for us *in Christ*. Central to God's eternal counsels concerning creation, central to God's work of providence, and central to all truly and systematically rational human knowledge of the world is the person and work of Jesus Christ, who is at once fully and truly eternal and historical.

Conversion to a faith-seeking-understanding program is futile for the purpose of worldview knowledge, much less personal salvation, unless this faith consists in personal knowledge of the triune God in Christ. It is, of course, beyond our natural

---

89. Van Til, *Introduction to Systematic Theology*, 261. Here Van Til is quoting Westminster Confession of Faith 2.1.

capacity to possess this faith. Faith is wrought in us by the regenerative work of the Holy Spirit. And make no mistake: this work in us is supernatural. As John Calvin puts it in one of the most splendid passages in his 1559 *Institutes*: "Now we shall possess a right definition of faith if we call it a firm and certain knowledge of God's benevolence toward us, founded upon the truth of the freely given promise in Christ, both revealed to our minds and sealed upon our hearts by the Holy Spirit."[90]

It would be befitting, then, to conclude this book by engaging with Kant on our most cherished knowledge of the person and work of our Lord and Savior. While Kant's account of the faith-knowledge distinction is, from a Reformed perspective, one of the most fundamental defects of his philosophy, its "greatest difficulty" is admittedly the problem of the atonement.[91] Although the greater emphasis of Kant's rational soteriology is on the problem of sanctification, he acknowledges the centrality of the problem of justification, of which the atonement is part and parcel.

We saw in chapter 2 that Kant's view of sin is deeply informed by Protestantism. He understands sin in terms of retributory, rather than distributive, justice. Moral guilt "is not a *transmissible* obligation . . . like . . . a monetary debt."[92] Kant explicitly states that "satisfaction must be rendered to the highest justice, before which someone punishable can never go unpunished."[93]

The question is: without knowing the Son, who bore the wrath of God at Golgotha; without the inward illumination of the Holy Spirit, who convicts us of our guilt; and without the written Word that reveals to us the God that *is*—not just the

90. John Calvin, *Institutes of the Christian Religion*, ed. John T. McNeill, trans. Ford Lewis Battles, 2 vols. (Philadelphia: Westminster Press, 1960), 3.2.7, 1:551.

91. Kant, *Religion*, 80.

92. Kant, *Religion*, 80 (italics original).

93. Kant, *Religion*, 81.

God that *ought to be*: how are we even able to understand the true meaning of the infinity of our guilt?

Historic Protestantism confesses faith in God's providential revelation in both world history and redemptive history. On this basis, we profess knowledge of an infinitely holy Judge who hates all sins. We understand human guilt in relation to this Judge. We know by faith that redemptive history is the axis of world history and that Christ is the center of redemptive history. We gaze, then—by faith and not by sight—on the Man at Golgotha on whom God's wrath was poured out, the Man who is also very God in one unabridged person. Only by this work of propitiation do we truly understand the severity of our guilt and the punishment it deserves.

Kant, by contrast, holds that divine-human relations are beyond the bounds of both theoretical and practical reason. Humans can never know the God that *is*; they can only postulate some god that *ought to be*. The "extravagant relation" between human beings and the supreme being that *ought to be* is an illusory thought "of which we understand nothing."[94] Yet Kant still wants to philosophically maintain his very Christian belief that human guilt is infinite. So he attributes this infinity to the universality of evil in the attitude and maxims of human beings.

It is not at all clear how *universality* translates to *infinity*, and Kant does not offer any satisfactory explanation. These are obviously different concepts. The fundamental laws of logic, for instance, are *universally* true, but it makes no sense to describe them as *infinitely* true. Or a mathematical function may approach infinity toward an asymptote, but it makes no sense to say that this function becomes universal at the asymptote—the universality and infinity of a function are different notions.

Kant in fact applies this confusion of universality with infinity

94. Kant, *Religion*, 70.

to a more central soteriological notion, namely, the infinite punishment of the sinner, which must be executed. He is right that in the case of criminal offenses, justice cannot be satisfied until the offender is properly punished. His solution, as we saw in chapter 2, is the notion of a union of attitudes with the Son of God.

Within the bounds of pure reason, of course, Kant cannot claim knowledge of the ontological Trinity. The Son of God has to be allegorically understood as humanity in the state of moral perfection. The attitude of the morally perfect human is such that he willfully sacrifices his happiness in order to fulfill his moral duties. This sacrifice, according to Kant, constitutes the infinite punishment that the sinner deserves.

Yet he does not explain *how* this sacrifice can be in any way infinite. The only way to make this intelligible at all is, again, to capitalize on the deceptive similarity between *infinity* and *universality*. It nevertheless remains unclear how the sacrifices associated with the change of moral attitudes constitute punishment commensurate with one's guilt.

First, although the change in moral attitudes *ought to be* universal, it cannot, as Kant himself concedes, *be* universal, because perfect transformation is beyond human capabilities. Second, experience tells us that the righteous do not always and necessarily suffer for being righteous. The transformation of moral attitudes is not necessarily painful, and thus it cannot be thought of as necessarily constituting any form of punishment. Third, upon the premises of retributory criminal justice, it is obvious that the requirements of the moral law are not satisfied by the offender's moral transformation, however much pain such a transformation may inflict on the guilty.

There is perhaps a ready answer in Kant's system to the first objection above. We noted in chapter 2 that Kant attempts to bridge the gap between the *is* and the *ought to be* of his moral religion by the notion of *hope* in divine grace. He defines *grace* as God's assistance in our endeavors to fulfill our moral vocation. Grace makes up for what we cannot achieve by our own powers in the process of sanctification.

Yet what Kant says about the role of grace in justification and atonement effectively amounts to nothing. There is certainly no gracious intervention that assists us in *being* punished, when we *ought to be* punished in accordance with an infinitely severe verdict. The problem of the satisfaction of the supreme justice, then, remains unresolved in Kant's moral religion.

Professor John Hare pinpoints the reason of the failure of Kant's translation of revealed soteriology to a soteriology of pure reason. Kant failed "because of his initial premise that the Son of God should be understood as mankind in its moral perfection."[95] This premise is in fact "a symptom . . . of a larger mistake in Kant": he is "too restrictive about what moral thinking is like."[96] Biblical faith plays only a peripheral role in the inner circle of rational religion, enclosed by the outer circle of revealed religion where biblical faith is truly at home.

Evangelical Christians, urges Professor Hare, should stand "against some things Kant says" about "Scripture as the vehicle of rational religion."[97] Kant thinks that Scripture and revealed religion are only de facto necessary for rational religion; they are not de jure necessary. When a morally perfect society is established on earth, Scripture and, along with it, faith in the historical person and work of Christ will no longer be necessary. This pure rationalist (I am with Professor Hare on interpreting Kant as a pure rationalist: see chapter 2) understanding of special revelation, part and parcel of Kant's faith-knowledge

95. Hare, *Moral Gap*, 270.
96. Hare, *Moral Gap*, 270.
97. John Hare, "Karl Barth, American Evangelicals, and Barth," in *Karl Barth and American Evangelicalism*, ed. Bruce McCormack and Clifford Anderson (Grand Rapids: Eerdmans, 2011), 85.

disjunction, is precisely the root of the ultimate failure of his moral religion.

Kant is well in agreement with mainstream Reformed theology, however, in his view that the punishable cannot go unpunished if supreme justice is to be satisfied. There were, of course, dissents among historic Reformed theologians on this topic, and even greater discord in the broader Latin tradition. John Owen correctly reports that according to the views of Augustine, Calvin, and "divers schoolmen," the punishable can in theory be forgiven and go unpunished by the sheer will of God.[98] The early Owen himself asserted a so-called hypothetical necessity of the satisfaction of divine justice, the view that punishment of the sinner is necessary, only upon the premise that it is God's decree to "manifest his glory . . . by the way of vindicative justice."[99]

Owen's later view, however, accords with mainstream Reformed doctrine: "punitive justice is natural to God, and necessary as to its egresses respecting sin."[100] This is indeed in line with the official position of Dort:

> God is not only supremely merciful, but also supremely just. And his justice requires (as he has revealed himself in his Word), that our sins committed against his infinite majesty should be punished, not only with temporal, but with eternal punishment, both in body and soul; which we cannot escape, unless satisfaction be made to the justice of God. (Canons of Dort, 2.1)

In other words, the punishable cannot go unpunished, ultimately because of God's natural justice that is immutable, and not just because God says so.

98. John Owen, *The Death of Death in the Death of Christ*, in *The Works of John Owen*, ed. William Goold, 23 vols. (Edinburgh: Banner of Truth, 1967), 10:275.
99. Owen, *Death of Death in the Death of Christ*, 10:205.
100. John Owen, *A Dissertation on Divine Justice*, in *Works*, 10:488.

Owen's argument represents the thrust of the rationale behind this mainline Reformed position: "He who cannot but hate all sin cannot but punish sin; for to hate sin is, as to the affection, to will to punish it, and as to the effect, the punishment itself. And to be unable not to will the punishment of sin is the same with the necessity of punishing it; for he who cannot but will to punish sin cannot but punish it."[101] Charles Hodge's exposition of the Reformed position is incisive:

> Expiation and propitiation are correlative terms. The sinner, or his guilt is expiated; God, or justice, is propitiated. Guilt must, from the nature of God, be visited with punishment, which is the expression of God's disapprobation of sin. Guilt is expiated . . . by satisfaction, i.e., by vicarious punishment. God is thereby rendered propitious, i.e., it is now consistent with his nature to pardon and bless the sinner. Propitious and loving are not convertible terms. God is love. He loved us while sinners, and therefore satisfaction was rendered. Satisfaction or expiation does not awaken love in the divine mind. It only renders it consistent with his justice that God should exercise his love towards transgressors of his law.[102]

This line of thought reflects Reformed orthodoxy's commitment to (1) the historic, catholic doctrine of the immutability of God's essence, and (2) the mainstream Reformed understanding of God's freedom and sovereignty, not as caprice of the will, but as the perfect correspondence of God's will and actions to his inward essence.

Interestingly, this mainline Reformed view of freedom, contrasted to Luther's more voluntaristic view, is the one that Kant

101. Owen, *Dissertation on Divine Justice*, 10:550.
102. Charles Hodge, *Systematic Theology*, 3 vols. (Grand Rapids: Eerdmans, 1989), 2:78.

formally adopted. As we saw in chapter 2, Kant rejects both the deterministic position that all acts of the will are predetermined by nature and the indeterministic conception of freedom as capricious choice. True freedom is *autonomy*—a much-misunderstood notion among both Christian and secularist readers. Kantian autonomy does not treat humanity as the measure of all things. Rather, it presupposes God's general revelation in human reason. Autonomy (per Kant) is, on the supposition of negative freedom (the freedom of choice), our willful act of imposing the universal moral law on ourselves.

We may even venture to say, based on some of Kant's explicit assumptions, that he thinks we are warranted in applying this view of freedom to God. Theoretical reason is capable of transcendentally demonstrating that the image of a capricious tyrant is inconsistent with the rational concept of God. Although transcendental theology cannot ascertain God's existence, it can at least tell us that he is, by conceptual definition, immutable. It seems reasonable to surmise that for Kant, the immutability of the moral law and its requirement of penal justice are grounded in the very nature of the supreme legislator that *ought to be*.

The fundamental defect of Kant's atonement theory, again, lies in the ontological and epistemic gulf between the *is* and the *ought to be*. Reformed theology grounds all human knowledge in special revelation. Calvin famously compared special revelation to a pair of spectacles through which we gaze on general revelation with our otherwise impaired vision. General revelation, to be sure, is perspicuous, but human reason is fallen. We know that *God is*, not by pure reason, but by special revelation. *God is* is the very name by which Yahweh introduced himself to Moses: *Ehyeh Asher Ehyeh*—perhaps best translated as "I am *I* Aм" (Ex. 3:14). The immutable being of God is supremely revealed to us in Jesus Christ, God the Son, who never ceased to be God even in his becoming human. He, in his flesh-becoming, revealed his eternally immutable essence with words unmistakable: "before Abraham was, I am" (John 8:58).

Without knowing Jesus Christ as truly and fully God and human in one unabridged second person of the Trinity, there is no way for us to truly understand the absolute necessity of penal satisfaction of divine justice. All biblical statements of the irrevocability of God's righteous wrath point to and culminate in the work of Christ at Golgotha. Because Jesus of Nazareth and God the Son is one person, we must confess that the Son himself died on the cross, just as we must confess that Mary is not only the mother of Christ, but truly the God-bearer. And by faith in the Son, whose person is of infinite worth, who bore God's wrath at Golgotha, we come to understand, through the price that he has paid, the infinity of our guilt. Thus the Canons of Dort: "The death of the Son of God is the only and most perfect sacrifice and satisfaction for sin; and is of infinite worth and value, abundantly sufficient to expiate the sins of the whole world" (2.3).

Of course, Kant is right that our guilt is not transmissible like a monetary debt. When the Bible teaches the nonimputation of sin (e.g., 2 Cor. 5:19) and the transfer of our guilt to Christ (e.g., v. 21), does it not portray God as a whimsical dictator? If it violates God's natural justice for him to forgive sinners without due punishment, would it not be even more blasphemous to say that he can, by the caprice of his will, decide to inflict infinite punishment on the one who knew no sin?

These questions essentially sum up Osiander's objections to the Lutheran doctrine of justification in the sixteenth century, and Calvin's rejoinder to Osiander has been the basic consensus among Reformed theologians since. Calvin agrees with Osiander that a legal fiction, as it were, is not sufficient for the atonement of sin because of the "axiom" that "the wrath of God rests upon all so long as they continue to be sinners."[103] To avoid rendering God a capricious tyrant who calls the innocent guilty and allows the guilty to go unpunished, Calvin bases his understanding of justification on the biblical notion of our mystical (i.e., real and not just nominal, albeit beyond physical sensibility) union with Christ. Because we are really made one with Christ, what is Christ's really becomes ours, and what is ours really becomes his.

In his construal of atonement and justification, Calvin accords to the "mystical union . . . the highest degree of importance."[104] When Christ accomplished propitiation on the cross, he was punished as one who truly bore our guilt. When God declares us righteous, we are truly clothed with Christ's righteousness.

Bavinck summarizes Calvin's view: "On account of our sins, we are indeed objects of God's wrath, writes Calvin, 'but because the Lord wills not to lose what is his in us, out of his own kindness he still finds something to love.'"[105] Bavinck is perfectly in line with mainstream Reformed orthodoxy when he explains that "this is not to be construed as if at the moment of Christ's sacrifice, God all at once changed his disposition and mood. For in God there is no variation or shadow due to change."[106] Indeed, Bavinck stands firm on the classical doctrine of divine impassibility and the Reformed doctrine of divine accommodation:

> When Scripture speaks of God's wrath and of his reconciliation with us, it does not speak untruth, yet it speaks in terms of our human capacity to understand. There is no change in God's being or essence but there is in the relation in which he stands to his creatures. Nor does he put himself in relation to his creatures as though they in any way existed outside him, but he

103. Calvin, *Institutes*, 3.11.21, 1:751.
104. Calvin, *Institutes*, 3.11.10, 1:737.
105. Bavinck, *Reformed Dogmatics*, 3:448.
106. Bavinck, *Reformed Dogmatics*, 3:448–49.

himself puts all things and all humans in those relations to himself that he eternally and unalterably wills and precisely in the manner and moment of time in which they occur in reality.[107]

Against post-Kantian idealist solutions to the problem of reconciliation, Bavinck clarifies that God "reconciles himself by the sacrifice of the cross, not in a patripassianistic or pantheistic sense as though he reconciles himself with himself and reconciliation were an immanent process in the life of God."[108] Idealists such as Hegel who recognized the failure of Kant's atonement theory were quick to invent a kind of process-trinitarian doctrine of reconciliation according to which God, in the process of becoming God, experiences self-alienation in order to reconcile himself to himself. According to this theory, God becomes truly and fully God only when human consciousness comes to comprehend its essential oneness with the mind of God.

In this family of post-Kantian soteriology, the Kantian demands for moral perfection and penal satisfaction of the supreme justice as criteria of our salvation are lifted. Salvation becomes humankind's attainment of so-called absolute freedom, in which individual rights, freedom, dignity, and identity are dissolved in what Bavinck calls a "deadly bath of uniformity."[109] This is a kind of reconciliation that "erase[s] the boundaries" between different natures within creation—"heaven and earth, matter and spirit, soul and body, man and animal," etc.—as well as the qualitative difference between "Creator and creature."[110]

This post-Kantian soteriology was developed in different directions in modernity. Both the idealist and materialist heirs of this historicist soteriology created savior-figures within this

---

107. Bavinck, *Reformed Dogmatics*, 3:449.
108. Bavinck, *Reformed Dogmatics*, 3:449.
109. Bavinck, *Reformed Dogmatics*, 2:435.
110. Bavinck, *Reformed Dogmatics*, 2:435.

world. Political entities such as the Third Reich and the Soviet Union, as well as individuals such as Hitler and Stalin, were idolized as embodiments of the Absolute and entrusted with the salvation of the world.

Modern Christian soteriology has often been tempted to choose between Kantian transcendence and post-Kantian immanence. The former regards the incarnation as beyond the bounds of knowledge; the latter identifies God the Son with historical activity. Dogmaticians such as Hodge and Bavinck are especially valuable against this milieu. Unwavering in their commitment to Chalcedonian Christology and historic Reformed soteriology, they are able to counter both Kantian positivism and post-Kantian historicism with distinctively modern rigor.

Of course, not all Christians are called to be dogmaticians, and not all dogmaticians are called to engage with modern philosophy. Bavinck and Hodge are, needless to say, exceptional cases in the history of Reformed dogmatics. While very few, if any, of us today are endowed with the gift to develop the philosophical acumen that they exemplify, there is something about them that all Christians can learn from.

They, like Schleiermacher, find the starting point of their theological inquiries in genuine knowledge of God in Jesus Christ at the initial stage of faith. Hodge acknowledges that "Schleiermacher retained all his life" his "reverence for Christ," and that "his philosophy, his historical criticism, everything, he was willing to make bend to the great aim of preserving to himself that cherished object of reverence and love."[111] What sets Hodge and Bavinck apart from Schleiermacher is that the former make a conscious effort to be guided and regulated by the perspicuous text of Scripture and the confessional orthodoxy of the Reformed churches in their quest for theological understanding.

---

111. Hodge, *Systematic Theology*, 2:440.

Genuinely Christian answers to Kant are, as Bavinck and Hodge have shown, readily available in historic Reformed theology as well as the broader orthodoxy of the Christian churches. The one catholic church through the ages has confessed knowledge of God in Jesus Christ, and this is the treasury of biblical wisdom that God has given to all his children. Bavinck and Hodge were great historians of doctrine before they became great dogmaticians. This is also the case for anyone who aspires to be a good theologian, for the simple reason that God ordained the church of the ages to be the "pillar and buttress of the truth" (1 Tim. 3:15).

We need to realize, however, that Bavinck and Hodge, as well as Kuyper, Dooyeweerd, Van Til, Geerhardus Vos, B. B. Warfield, and other great theologians of old, have gone to be with that splendid cloud of witnesses. New philosophical challenges to our faith abound today, often in more sophisticated forms than Kantian and post-Kantian thought. I freely admit that with my academic limitations, I am not equipped to deal with the challenges from, say, Ludwig Wittgenstein or Jacques Derrida. Still, my faith remains a firm and certain knowledge of God in Christ.

We might not be able to understand all philosophies, let alone answer them all. While it is indeed immensely helpful for Christians to engage with the wisdom of this world, let us be reminded by that cloud of witnesses that there is no salvation apart from Christ, and that only knowledge of God in Christ leads to true knowledge of all things. Faith in Christ is the *sine qua non* of true wisdom. Kant thinks that revealed religion will ultimately make way for rational religion, but Scripture tells us that this is impossible until kingdom (literally) come. Then the wisdom of the world will make way for our sight of the personal glory of God in Christ, which has already been revealed to us through faith by the Holy Spirit.

Now we have received not the spirit of the world, but the Spirit who is from God, that we might understand the things freely given us by God. And we impart this in words not taught by human wisdom but taught by the Spirit, interpreting spiritual truths to those who are spiritual.

The natural person does not accept the things of the Spirit of God, for they are folly to him, and he is not able to understand them because they are spiritually discerned. The spiritual person judges all things, but is himself to be judged by no one. "For who has understood the mind of the Lord so as to instruct him?" But we have the mind of Christ. (1 Cor. 2:12–15)

GLOSSARY

Navigating through the sea of technical terms in Kant's writings can be a frustrating experience. The following glossary covers some of his basic vocabulary. Its scope is inevitably limited. Howard Caygill's *Dictionary* (see Recommended Reading) would prove to be a reliable gyroscope while at sea—it is the one I use for serious lexical study. Most of the time, however, the reader might prefer briefer definitions. A number of glossaries are available on the Internet. In my teaching, I have relied on the one that Stephen Palmquist published on his professional website. His other glossary, found at the end of *Kant's Critical Religion* (see Recommended Reading), is especially helpful for understanding the theological dimension of Kant's philosophy. Note that Palmquist's definitions are offered within a particular framework of interpretation (called "System of Perspectives") and may appear different from ones offered in other glossaries, including this one.

Note: The following abbreviations are used in this glossary. The pagination corresponds to the translations and editions listed in the bibliography.

CPJ	*Critique of the Power of Judgment*
CPR	*Critique of Pure Reason*
CPrR	*Critique of Practical Reason*
GMM	*Groundwork of the Metaphysics of Morals*
RBBR	*Religion within the Bounds of Bare Reason*

analysis. A method of philosophizing inherited from Leibnizian and Wolffian metaphysics, aimed at determining a concept or representation by comparing it to its opposite, in order to demonstrate the reasons behind its truthfulness. Analyses are useful for the clarification of concepts or representations, but they do not amplify knowledge. See **determination.** Compare **synthesis.**

a posteriori. In the tradition of medieval scholasticism down to early-modern rationalism, descriptive of logical demonstrations from effects to cause. Wolff retains this definition. In Hume, *a posteriori* describes a mode of reasoning that presupposes experience. Kant basically adopts Hume's definitions, but makes some subtle yet important clarifications. The terms *a priori* and *a posteriori*, in Kant, primarily qualify cognitions. An *a posteriori* cognition is "that which is merely borrowed from experience," that is, that which is "cognized . . . only empirically" (*CPR*, A2).

appearance. The aspect of an object that is experienced by us in and through space and time. For experience to be possible, external things must appear to us. The *appearance* (*Erscheinung*, to be distinguished from *Schein*, by which Kant means illusion) of a thing, transcendentally speaking, is the very object of experience. In other words, what is given to the mind through sensibility is not the ontological substance of the object, but rather its appearance. There is a difference between *appearance* and phenomenon. Appearances are representations, conditioned by spatiotemporality, that precede our conceptual use of the understanding, while phenomena are representations of the objects of experiences that ensue from the intellectual comparison of appearances. While appearance is contrasted to the thing in itself, the noumenon-phenomenon distinction is a closely related but somewhat distinct binary. Sensibility as described above is an overall (though not completely) passive faculty: it makes a representation only when it is acted on by an external object that appears to us, for our cognitive faculties are incapable of originating appearances. See **transcendental.**

a priori. In medieval scholasticism and early-modern rationalism, descriptive of logical demonstrations from cause to effects. Hume redefines *a priori* as describing a mode of reasoning that does not presuppose experience. Following Hume, Kant gives to *a priori* cognitions the basic definition of that which is independent of experience. Kant ascribes to *a priori* cognitions three basic criteria: (1) universality, (2) necessity, and (3) purity. Universality is conjoined with necessity, and they are defined in terms of independence from experience: "universal cognitions, which at the same time have the character of inner necessity, must be clear and certain for themselves, independently of experience; hence one calls them *a priori* cognitions" (*CPR,* A1). For the purity of *a priori* cognitions, see **pure.** Compare *a posteriori.*

autonomy. The third formula of the categorical imperative: it is "the idea *of the will of every rational being as a universally legislating will*" (*GMM,* 43 [italics original]). Autonomy is the very "ground of the dignity of a human and of every rational nature" (*GMM,* 43). Kant's notion of autonomy is often misunderstood as a state of independence from God. There is some truth to this secularist misreading of

Kantian autonomy. The word is composed of the Greek *auto* ("self") and *nomos* ("law"), by which Kant means "self-legislation." In his earlier works in the Critical period, there are strong suggestions that *autonomy* means human self-legislation apart from God's revelation. His mature understanding of God as supreme moral legislator outside the human being is not clearly spelled out in these works—sometimes it is even denied. In the *Groundwork*, for instance, human autonomy means that "every rational being, as an end in itself, must be able to view itself as at the same time universally legislating with regard to any law whatsoever to which it may be subject, because it is just this fittingness of its maxims for universal legislation that marks it out as an end in itself" (*GMM*, 49). One reason why Kant's discourse on autonomy is often understood as a secularist one may be that in his earlier works, he speaks of human moral agents as the "lawgiving members of a kingdom of morals" (*CPrR*, 68). He even considers attribution of supreme lawgiving agency to the "will of God" a position of "heteronomy" (*CPrR*, 54). But he modifies this position in the third *Critique*, where he conceptually identifies God as not only the supreme determining ground of our moral will, but also "the highest morally legislative author" (*CPJ*, 320). The rationality of faith in God as the supreme moral legislator lies in this: "given the constitution of the faculty of our reason, we could not even make comprehensible the kind of purposiveness related to the moral law and its object that exists in this final end without an author and ruler of the world who is at the same time a moral legislator" (*CPJ*, 320). In this light, Kantian autonomy should be understood as the noncoerced will to abide by the supreme moral law revealed to human reason. See **dignity; idea; maxim.**

beautiful, the. An objective quality that induces a certain feeling of pleasure in a disinterested (impartial) observer. Kant was already concerned with the aesthetic notions of the beautiful and the sublime in his early career. In a short treatise dating from 1764, titled *Observations on the Feelings of the Beautiful and the Sublime* (*Beobachtungen über das Gefühl des Schönen und Erhabenen*), he offers a pre-Critical defense of the objectivity of these feelings. It is in the third *Critique* (1790) that he offers a Critical account of these aesthetic notions. According to the third *Critique, the beautiful* (*das Schöne*) gives rise to an immediate feeling of pleasure, and it "pleases without [subjective] interest," for it is a symbol of the moral good (*CPJ*, 227). When I call *Mona Lisa* beautiful, for example, it is because it carries certain artistic forms—perspective, colors, lighting, and so on—that immediately please me. The beautiful does not please my senses—I do not really sense beauty as an empirical object; nor does it please "in accordance with a concept of the understanding," for the feeling of the beautiful is immediate (*CPJ*, 150). The pleasure associated with the beautiful is purely positive. See **concept; understanding.**

categorical imperative. An end in itself, rather than the achievement of an end, defined by three formulae: (1) the formula of universality (the law of nature); (2) the formula of humanity; and (3) the formula of autonomy. The first of these is central to the definition of the categorical imperative. It is, in fact, the very imperative itself: "there is . . . only a single categorical imperative, and it is this: act only according to that maxim through which you can at the same time will that it become a universal law" (*GMM*, 33). For more information on the second and third formulae, see **dignity.** Also see **maxim.** Compare **hypothetical imperative.**

categories. Pure concepts of the intellect with which we understand the order of the external world. Kant identifies four major categories: (1) quantity (unity, plurality, totality); (2) quality (reality, negation, limitation); (3) relation (inherence and subsistence, causality and dependence, community); (4) modality (possibility-impossibility, existence-nonexistence, necessity-contingency). This table of categories is reminiscent of but somewhat different from Aristotle's. Kant explicitly follows Aristotle in calling the pure concepts of the intellect *categories*. In the Aristotelian tradition, the categories constitute a built-in structure of the mind that is universal to all human beings. This structure is analogous to, though not identical with, the order of the external world. Kant moves beyond Aristotle in grounding the formulation of the categories on the principle of judgment. The categories are intended to be an exhaustive account of the logical functions of the understanding, which we apply to objects given to the mind to form judgments. All the categories are there in our minds, and unlike the case of the imagination, we are conscious of how our minds operate with the categories. Unlike empirical concepts, which are innumerable because we never stop imaginatively synthesizing new concepts from contingent experiences, the categories are numerically exhaustible because they are in our minds, and the conscious functions of our minds are limited. See page 54 for Kant's table of categories.

cognition. One of a family of representations that feature prominently in the first *Critique*, defined in simple terms as the process by which we make sense of sensible things. This process is perceptive and objective. It is perceptive in that it is a conscious representation, and objective in that it is directed toward the object. Cognition gives rise to judgments, which are the smallest units of knowledge. In order to make sense of sensible things, two preconditions must be fulfilled: (1) some sensible thing of which to make sense must be given to our minds, and (2) our minds must possess something *a priori* with which to make sense of the sensible things given. Fulfilling the first precondition here is the task of the cognitive faculty of sensibility. The second precondition is achieved by the faculty of understanding. Note that sometimes Kant uses *cognition* in a looser sense, such that a sensible intuition can also be called a *cognition*. Also see **theoretical and practical cognitions.**

concept. The primary representation of the understanding. Concepts are contrasted to (sensible) intuitions in two important respects. First, although concepts and intuitions are both objective (i.e., they address objects), intuitions are singular and particular, while concepts refer to a plurality of objects in their universality. Second, intuitions are immediate, while concepts operate in indirect and complex manners. We use concepts of various sorts to synthetically represent new concepts. Kant distinguishes between empirical concepts and pure concepts. Compare **sensible intuition.**

constitutive principle. A postulate that we can ascertain by reason, so long as this postulate provides a "certain determinate condition" that is "absolutely necessary" for what we know to be true and real (*CPR*, A632/B660). Kant claims in the second *Critique* that in our practical reason, the ideas of God, freedom, and immortality become immanent and constitutive to us. The practical use of reason provides a ground for the extension of theoretical reason to objects that are otherwise transcendent and unknowable. See **principle.** Compare **regulative principle.**

determination. The reason underlying the actuality of a factual possible and the reason underlying the exclusion of its counterfactual possible. Kant's definition of *determination*

(*Bestimmen*) builds on Wolff's use of the term. Wolff envisions reality in terms of his philosophy of possibles. The reality of life on earth, for instance, is a factual possible; it is also possible, though counterfactual, that there is no life on earth. That there is life on earth not only is possible and factual, but also becomes determinate when we give a reason not only why there is life on earth, but also why the contradictory possible is excluded. Kant takes this definition further by proposing the notion of a *complete determination*: something is completely determinate when the sum total of all its possible predicates is considered in relation to the contradictory opposite of each predicate. Kant retains the rationalist view that reality is ultimately rational and not contingent. This means that there must be ultimate reasons why some possibles are factual and why some are not. Hegel would later transform Kant's architectonic notion of *Bestimmen* into an organic notion of *Bestimmung* (also translated as "determination"), such that truth and reality are no longer characterized by being and nonbeing (*is* and *is not*), but rather by the dialectical process of alienation and reconciliation.

dignity. The inalienable core of humanity qua humanity, with an inner worth that is immeasurable, whereby every human individual as a rational being should be treated *"always at the same time as an end,* [and] *never merely as a means"* (*GMM*, 41 [italics original]). This notion of humanity—and all rational beings—as an end and not merely a means toward an end lies at the core of the celebrated Kantian notion of human *dignity* (*Würde*). We are members of the "kingdom of ends [*Reich der Zwecke*]," in which everything has either a price or an "inner worth" called *dignity* (*GMM*, 46). Something that has a price is exchangeable with some other thing of equal worth. Dignity, on the other hand, is that inner worth "elevated above any price, and hence allows of no equivalent," for it is an end in itself, and not a means toward another end (*GMM*, 46). There are, of course, things within the realm of human existence that have prices. "Skill and diligence in work have a market price; wit, lively imagination, and humor have a fancy price" (*GMM*, 46). Things pertaining to our moral nature, however, such as "fidelity in promising and benevolence from principles (not from instinct)," have an "inner worth" that is priceless (*GMM*, 46). Human beings have dignity precisely because we are rational beings endowed with moral reason. Autonomy is the ground of human dignity. See **principle.**

discursivity. The interplay between sensibility and understanding that makes the objectivity of empirical knowledge possible. Kant takes for granted that the fact that we can think the world means that the world must be capable of being thought. This two-way traffic means that human cognition must be discursive (*diskursiv*): it necessarily involves an interplay between sensibility and understanding, two cognitive faculties that are distinct from each other. These two cognitive faculties give rise to different types of representations. Kant does not see any need to justify the basic assumption of the discursivity of human cognition: we have to start from here; otherwise, we cannot make sense of the fact that we do make sense of many matters of fact. In his own famous words, "the attempt to think them [objects of experience] . . . will provide a splendid touchstone of what we assume as the altered method of our way of thinking"—"for they *must be* capable of being thought" (*CPR*, Bxvii [italics added]). The *discursivity thesis* features prominently in the Henry Allison school of Kant interpretation.

empirical concept. A concept represented from experience, which is *a posteriori*. There is, of course, quite a gap between individual intuitions and their synthesis into an empirical concept. The word *synthesis* here refers generally to the mental act of gathering and conjoining different representations, in order to represent them in one cognition. In the synthesis of manifold intuitions into a concept, the act is spontaneous. The cognitive faculty responsible for syntheses in general is the power of imagination. Compare **pure concept.**

empirical intuition. An intuition that relates to objects through sensations within the representations of space and time. In this way, even sensibility—not just the intellect—involves something pure and *a priori*. Compare **intellectual intuition; pure intuition; sensible intuition.**

faith (belief). "*Habitus*, not . . . *actus*": "reason's moral way of thinking in the affirmation of that which is inaccessible for theoretical cognition" (*CPJ*, 335). Kant differentiates *faith/belief* (*Glaube*) from knowledge and opinion. Because the object of faith is beyond theoretical cognition, faith does not qualify as knowledge. Yet faith is rational, insofar as it makes a postulation that is necessary for making sense of the realities or possibilities that are known to us. In this sense, faith differs from "opinion": the latter is characterized by mere "credulity," and is entirely groundless, while faith is characterized by rational certainty (*CPJ*, 335). The constitutive postulation of God's existence "in relation to the intelligibility of an object given us by the moral law (the highest good), and consequently of a need for practical purposes, . . . can be called belief [*Glaube*] and, indeed, a pure rational belief since pure reason alone (in its theoretical as well as in its practical use) is the source from which it springs" (*CPrR*, 102). Kant's express intention in his Critical works is to critique human reason, not faith; and his intention in the critique of human reason, as he explicitly states in the preface to the second edition of the first *Critique*, is "to deny knowledge in order to make room for faith" (*CPR*, Bxxx). See **postulate; pure reason.**

freedom. Along with God and immortality, one of the three metaphysical ideas discussed in the second *Critique*. In the first *Critique*, Kant considers the dialectic between determinism and indeterministic freedom. According to the former, "everything . . . happens solely in accordance with the laws of nature," and there is no genuine freedom of the will (*CPR*, A445/B473). The latter, by contrast, insists on a "lawless faculty of freedom" that precludes any adequate notion of "nature" (*CPR*, A449/B477). According to Kant, both views are transcendentally invalid, and the metaphysical idea of freedom remains an illusion within theoretical reason. When we transition to practical reason, however, this problem is purportedly resolved. Genuine, positive freedom, per Kant, is autonomy, which is knowing and doing what we ought to do: to abide by the universal law of our moral nature in every *choice* (*Willkür*) of the *will* (*Wille*). A will governed by *animal instinct* (*arbitrium brutus*) is not free. Only a will to carry out the categorical imperative given to our moral nature is genuinely free. The freedom of autonomy, then, presupposes negative freedom, which is noncoercion of the will. If the moral law were imposed on us, we would be under heteronomy (under the rule of another legislator), and thus not autonomous. See **transcendental.**

hypothetical imperative. An imperative that is not universally or absolutely valid. Its moral-rational validity is contingent on the end that it is aimed at achieving, and so it is not an end in itself. For instance, hard work is not an end in itself. It is good only if one works hard for a good end. Compare **categorical imperative.**

idea. A special species of pure concepts. Kant distinguishes between *idea* and concept. Causality and existence are examples of pure concepts of the understanding. Ideas, on the other hand, are pure concepts of reason, the cognitive faculty responsible for synthesizing judgments to form coherent systems of knowledge. Kant uses *idea* in dialogue with traditional metaphysics, particularly the rationalist notion of *innate ideas*. In the first *Critique*, he offers lengthy discussions of the ideas of the soul, the world, and God, in response to the Wolffian divisions of rational psychology, rational cosmology, and rational theology. Kant's basic claim is that traditional metaphysical treatments of these ideas fall short of synthetic *a priori* judgments and that in their analytic speculation, no determination about any of these ideas can be made. Rational cosmology, for instance, unavoidably falls into *antinomies*, a situation in which every predication of the idea (e.g., the existence of the world is caused) and its contradictory opposite (e.g., the world is uncaused and self-existent) can be proved by equally valid arguments or counterarguments.

ideal. The individual concretion of an idea, "that is, as an individual thing, determinable or even determined by the idea alone" (*CPR*, A568/B596). Kant gives simpler definitions of the terms in the third *Critique*: "Idea signifies, strictly speaking, a concept of reason, and ideal the representation of an individual being as adequate to an idea" (*CPJ*, 117). God, strictly speaking, is the only true ideal, though Kant also speaks of ideals such as that "of the beautiful," which he identifies as the concretion of the "archetype of taste" (A568/B596). See **beautiful, the; concept; reason; representation.**

idealism. The interpretation of a thing as a mere idea in the mind, denying the ascertainability of the objective existence of that thing in itself apart from the mind. The opposite of idealism is realism. To be a realist about something is to assert the reality of that thing in itself apart from the mind. It would be a grave mistake to simplistically label Kant as an idealist. Leaving aside scholarly debates, his intentions are explicit: he intends to be a transcendental idealist and an empirical realist. That is, he treats space and time as transcendentally ideal (though objectively real), in order to ensure that the objects of our experience are real. See **transcendental idealism.**

illusion (*Illusion; Schein*). The belief that we have determinate knowledge of the objects to which metaphysical ideas such as God supposedly refer. We innately possess ideas such as God, and the illusion that we cognize real objects to which these ideas refer arises from the very constitution of our intellectual and rational faculties. Kant compares the unavoidability of this kind of illusion to the way that, to our eyes, "the sea appears higher at the middle than at the shores" (*CPR*, A297/B353–A298/B354). Transcendental critique of our cognition reveals the core beliefs of rational metaphysics to be mere illusions.

imagination, power of (*Einbildungskraft*). The cognitive faculty responsible for syntheses in general. This function of the mind is for the most part subconscious, and Kant admits that we know precious little about how it works. We do know that it is there, however, because the synthesis of representations in the production of empirical concepts would not have been possible otherwise.

immanent. See **transcendent-immanent distinction.**

imperative. A proposition expressing a possible free action that realizes a certain end. Whereas theoretical reason is concerned with indicatives (*what is*), practical reason is preoccupied with imperatives (*what ought to be*). Kant distinguishes between two kinds of imperatives: hypothetical imperative and categorical imperative.

intellectual intuition. Immediate cognition or representation of an external object by the intellect alone. While Kant insists that all human intuitions are sensible, he also acknowledges that the kind of intellectual intuitions with which rationalist metaphysics sought to view the self, the world, and God can, in theory, exist as well. He juxtaposes intellectual intuitions to sensible intuitions. The former represents an object entirely *ex nihilo*, and does not depend on the existence of the object or its effect on the capacity to represent. In this sense, sensible intuitions are said to be derivative, while intellectual intuitions are said to be original. To say that God's intuition is intellectual is the same as saying that his intellect is intuitive, and his understanding immediate. There is no need for deduction or reflection in God's mind, nor does he need to experience matters of fact in order to know them, for he possesses immediate knowledge of all things. That is, God knows all things all at once, and his cognition is unconfined by space and time. Compare **empirical intuition; pure intuition.**

intuition (Latin: *intuitus*). At its most basic, immediate cognition or immediate representation. But what can we cognize immediately? Kant rejected the early-modern rationalist view that we use our intellect (Latin: *intellectio*) to intuit the external world, a view that assumes that the world is substantially intelligible, rather than sensible. For Kant, our intellect is incapable of intuiting anything, not even the spiritual substance of our thinking self. All human intuitions, says Kant, are sensible intuitions. When our capacity to represent is acted on by the appearances of external objects, a representation called *intuition* (*Anschauung*) arises as an immediate response mechanism of the cognitive faculty of sensibility. The German word *Anschauung* literally means "to look at" or "to gaze upon," and this literal meaning says a lot about what it expresses metaphorically. The act of looking at something is directed toward the object that is being looked at. As far as experience is concerned, an intuition is the immediate representation of an individual object to the mind. This representation is an act of the faculty of sensibility directed toward the object. The object appears to our senses, and we intuit it through sensation. Not all intuitions are empirical, however. Kant distinguishes between two kinds of sensible intuitions (intuitions pertaining to sensibility) that human beings can possess, namely, pure intuitions and empirical intuitions. See **intellectual intuition.**

judgment, power of. The cognitive faculty that serves as the judicial standpoint from which we, with reflecting uses of it, come to definite types of feelings associated with aesthetic and teleological realities out there. In the third *Critique*, Kant explores the cognitive faculty of the *power of judgment* (*Urteilskraft*), in an attempt to explain the rational objectivity of our feelings. Feelings such as pleasure, sorrow, and awe are associated with the power of judgment. When we judge something to be beautiful, sublime, or good, we exercise the power of judgment. In the reflecting use of the power of judgment, we are given something particular, such as the starry heavens, and then we work our way up to a universal under which the particular may be subsumed. When we reflect on the "starry heavens," a feeling of awe or reverence is aroused, and we call "the sight . . . sublime" (*CPJ*, 152). Aesthetic judgments pertain mainly to two kinds of objects: the beautiful and the sublime, which give rise to different types of feelings.

judgments. Combinations of concepts formed by the reflecting power of the cognitive faculty of understanding. A concept can be either *a priori* (independent of experience) or *a posteriori* (derived from experience). The formation of judgments from concepts can be either synthetic or analytic. Analytic judgments are propositions in which the predicate is already included in the subject (e.g., "all boys are male"): it serves to clarify the concept or representation, but does not amplify knowledge. Synthetic judgments, by contrast, are judgments of amplification: they are propositions in which the predicate provides new information not contained in the subject (e.g., "this cat is cheerful"). Synthetic *a posteriori* judgments combine empirical representations to render new information that is not necessarily true. By contrast, analytic *a priori* judgments are judgments of clarification about nonempirical representations. They are necessarily true, but do not lead us to knowledge of anything that we did not already know. Only synthetic *a priori* judgments—judgments of amplification that are nonempirical—give us knowledge of new information that is necessarily true. Human knowledge and science hinge on the very possibility of synthetic *a priori* judgments.

knowledge. Judgments or systems of judgments resulting from the combination of intuitions and concepts by the cognitive faculty of understanding. Kant sets knowledge apart from faith (belief) and opinion. An opinion is without any rational ground, while faith is rational belief that does not meet the criterion of knowledge. Kant distinguishes between two types of knowledge, the latter of which has often been overlooked in the scholarship, namely, knowledge pertaining to theoretical reason (*what is*) and knowledge pertaining to practical reason (*what ought to be*). God as the ideal of pure reason is an object of faith in the former (by virtue of being a regulative principle), but becomes an object of knowledge in the latter (as a constitutive principle). Cognition and concepts do not qualify as knowledge yet; they are merely the building blocks of knowledge. Judgments are the smallest units of knowledge. In the theoretical use of reason, judgments that constitute knowledge must meet the synthetic *a priori* criterion—this is so even for pure sciences such as arithmetic and geometry. Objects of empirical knowledge must be intuitable in the forms of space and time. See **synthetic *a priori* judgments.**

maxim. A principle of the will, which a person subjectively determines by her or his own reason as the standard for moral actions. Kant takes for granted the unity and coherence of the universal law, and the test for whether a maxim can become a universal law is to examine whether it accords with other universal moral laws of nature. The supreme moral vocation of humankind is "the restoration . . . of the purity of the moral law as the supreme basis of all our maxims" (*RBBR*, 52).

natural theology. Theology that thinks its object "through a concept which it borrows from nature (the nature of our soul) as the highest intelligence" (*CPR*, A631/B659). Whereas transcendental theology appeals to pure reason alone, natural theology resorts to experience. Natural theology as such, per Kant, cannot be truly theological on its own, for apart from transcendental concepts, it ultimately reduces God to nature. "If the empirically valid law of causality is to lead to an original being, then this would have to belong to the causal chain in objects of experience; but then it, like all appearances, would have to be conditioned" (*CPR*, A636/B664). What natural theology on its own renders, then, is "far from any concept of a highest being, because for us experience never offers us the greatest of all possible effects" (*CPR*, A637/B665). See **appearance.** Compare **rational theology; revealed theology.**

noumenon. The ontological substance of an object above and behind its phenomena. The term *noumenon* is often, but not always, used interchangeably with thing in itself. *Noumenon* stands in juxtaposition to phenomenon, which is an object of sensibility.

phenomenon. The aspect of an empirical object, conditioned by space and time, that is available to human knowledge. Sensibility represents to us an external object as it appears to our senses. What is given to the mind through sensibility is not the ontological substance of the object, but rather its appearance. There is a difference between appearances and phenomena. Appearances are representations that precede our conceptual use of the understanding, while representations of the objects of experiences that ensue from the intellectual comparison of appearances are called *phenomena*. According to the interpretation offered in this book, *appearance* (*Erscheinung*), derived from the verb *erscheinen*, is the movement through which the thing in itself reveals itself, as it were. By contrast, a noumenon is veiled by its phenomenon. The two binaries (noumena-phenomena distinction and the appearance of the thing in itself) form a dialectical process of self-manifestation through self-concealment.

postulate. A fundamental principle on which known facts and truths depend. Western philosophy has traditionally followed Aristotle in distinguishing between postulates and axioms. An axiom is a self-evident truth that is indemonstrable and yet theoretically constitutive. An example in Euclidian geometry is the axiom that the closest distance between two points in space is a straight line. Kant adopts the traditional definitions of *postulate* and *axiom* and incorporates them into his philosophy. In Kant, postulates, as regulative propositions in the theoretical use of reason, are immediately certain and yet indemonstrable. In the practical use of reason, postulates such as the existence of God become constitutive and demonstrable by a *reductio ad absurdum*. See **constitutive principle; practical reason; regulative principle; theoretical reason.**

power of imagination. See **imagination, power of.**

power of judgment. See **judgment, power of.**

practical reason. Reason that is concerned with what ought to be. In the practical use of reason, ideas such as God, freedom, and immortality become constitutive principles. As such, they become objects of knowledge. We know, for instance, that God ought to be, and that human beings ought to be free—something that we cannot ascertain in the theoretical use of reason—because these are postulates without which our universal moral vocation cannot be explained. Compare **pure reason; theoretical reason.**

predisposition. An innate property that cannot be extinguished. Kant distinguishes between *predisposition* (*Anlage*) and propensity (*Hang*). A propensity can "be thought (if it is good) as acquired, or (if it is evil) as brought upon the human being by himself" (*RBBR*, 50). Human beings are born with a natural predisposition to the good and a propensity to evil. This is roughly in line with the Latin Christian doctrine of original sin, according to which human beings are good by essential nature, and became sinful in acquiring an accidental nature through the fall. Kant states that "the human being . . . is created good," in the sense that "he is created for the good, and the original predisposition in the human being is good" (*RBBR*, 50).

principle. Simply understood, a logical and/or ontological starting point; a judgment that is immediately certain *a priori*. Kant uses *Prinzip* and *Grundsatz* interchangeably as his German rendering of the Latin philosophical term *principium*. The Latin term, in turn, is a translation of the Greek *archē*. Literally, *Grundsatz* means "ground proposition." A principle provides the ground on which other judgments may be demonstrated, while its certainty does not depend on these other judgments. Note that rational certainty does not necessarily imply knowledge. Faith is also characterized by rational certainty. A principle is constitutive when it is an object of knowledge, regulative when it is an object of faith. Kant distinguishes between the principles of pure understanding and the principles of practical reason. The categories and the principles of space and time are examples of the former. The autonomy of the will is a chief principle of practical reason. See **constitutive principle; regulative principle.**

propensity. "The subjective basis for the possibility of an inclination (habitual desire . . .) insofar as this possibility is contingent for humanity as such" (*RBBR*, 31). Kant distinguishes between *propensity* (*Hang*) and predisposition (*Anlage*). Predisposition to the good was given to humankind upon creation, and is essential to human nature. All fallen human beings are born with radical propensities to evil that cannot be extirpated. These evil propensities, however, are brought upon themselves. Human beings can also acquire propensities to the good in order to outweigh their evil propensities. Kant's definition of *propensity* serves to support his view that human beings must be held responsible for adopting evil maxims in their evil propensities through the negative freedom of *choice* (*Willkür*). His view of propensities as something accidental to human nature also serves to underscore his final aim in moral religion, namely, a conscious turning away from evil propensities and the subordination of one's propensities to the moral law in one's maxims and actions.

pure. Unmixed with experience. The word *pure (rein)* can have a variety of meanings in Kant's writings. Sometimes it is synonymous with *a priori,* but if *a priori* implies only the conditions of universality and necessity, then purity encompasses these conditions. There can be different degrees and types of purity. The adjective can qualify a number of nouns, such as cognition, intuition, concept, *rational* faith, reason, and *religion.*

pure concept. A concept that does not depend on experience. In addition to empirical concepts, Kant stresses that we must possess pure concepts. These include concepts such as *existence* and *causality,* which we possess prior to representing any actual object, or anything actually existent or caused. Such a concept is represented entirely *a priori,* and as such it is called a *pure concept.* The pure concepts of understanding are crucial for enabling synthetic judgments to be *a priori.* See **categories; synthetic *a priori* judgments.**

pure intuition. An intuition that is entirely unmixed with experience and serves as the *a priori* precondition for empirical intuitions. More precisely, pure intuitions are the representations of space and time as the very form of our sensible intuitions. Compare **intellectual intuition.**

pure reason *(reine Vernunft).* "That which contains the principles for cognizing something absolutely *a priori*" (*CPR* A11/B24). By pure, Kant basically means "unmixed with experience." See ***a priori;* cognition; reason.** Compare **practical reason; theoretical reason.**

rational theology (Latin: *theologia rationalis*). Cognition of God "from pure reason" (*CPR,* A631/B659). Kant's use of the term *rational theology* is derived from the Wolffian division of special metaphysics, namely, rational theology, rational cosmology, and rational psychology. Because God is the ideal of pure reason in whom no attribute is contingent, propositions describing God's attributes, such as "God is omnipotent," are all analytical. Such propositions are true by conceptual necessity, but they say nothing of God's existence. All existential predications are synthetic: "God exists" is a proposition that synthesizes two distinct concepts— God and existence. No synthetic proposition can be true by logical necessity. Analytic propositions about the idea of God, however, cannot be the determination of a real being, for determination necessarily involves synthetic judgments. In the theoretical use of reason, the idea of God becomes determinate to us only when it is measured against another object, but because God is the original and highest being, there is no being against which God's being can be measured. If God is indeed the only true ideal of pure reason— an idea of the highest rank—then it can never satisfy the criterion of determinacy (being affirmed or negated on the ground of an other). Therefore, cognition of God in rational theology is a mere illusion. See **synthetic *a priori* judgments; theology; theoretical reason.** Compare **natural theology; revealed theology; transcendental theology.**

realism. The position that something has its own reality apart from our perception. Realism is juxtaposed to idealism, which holds that we have access only to our own ideas of things without knowing whether these ideas correspond to actual existences outside our minds. Kant is a realist with regard to the objects of experience, and contends that empirical realism can be upheld only if we acknowledge the ideality of space and time as the transcendental forms of our experience.

reason. The higher cognitive faculty that synthesizes judgments (the smallest units of knowledge) to form coherent systems of knowledge. Many readers approaching Kant for the first time have the impression of a juxtaposition between pure reason and practical reason in his vocabulary. This confusion understandably arises from the titles of the first two *Critiques*—*Pure Reason* and *Practical Reason*. The reader should bear in mind, however, that practical reason can also be pure—it can cognize universal and necessary truths entirely *a priori*. Kant's dichotomy is between theoretical reason and practical reason, instead of the pure and the practical.

regulative principle. A logical and ontological starting point (this is the basic definition of a principle) that, among other possible starting points, directs the understanding to the highest degree of unity and coherence, but the validity of which we can never know for sure—not even by a *reductio ad absurdum*. A regulative principle "can be presupposed only as optional and contingent" (*CPR*, A632/B660). Compare **constitutive principle.**

representation *(Vorstellung)*. A generic term for all cognitive acts of the mind. Literally, the verb *vorstellen* means "to put forth." *Vorstellung*, in its everyday usage, can carry a number of designations, including "conception," "notion," "perception," "belief," "view," "presentation," and "introduction." The standard English translation of this term comes from Kant's own use of *Vorstellung* as the German equivalent of the Latin *repræsentatio*. Traditionally, *repræsentatio* refers generically to all the ways in which something is presented to the mind, and Kant adopts this basic definition. For Kant, conceptual representations can be *a priori* or *a posteriori*. A concept itself can also be called a *representation*. Kant's usage of the term breaks with the rationalist tradition in a significant way. In early-modern rationalism, *repræsentatio* is by definition *intellectual* (i.e., represented by the intellect). Taking seriously Hume's critique of rationalism without buying into Humean skepticism, Kant insists that although we must presuppose permanent substance as a principle (as opposed to something ontological) underlying the objects represented to our minds in space and time, our intellect is incapable of immediately grasping ontological substances. Objects can be represented to the mind only indirectly by our own cognitive faculties. Each external object is individually given to our minds through sensible experience, and our faculty of the understanding then gathers and processes these raw materials to give rise to cognition.

revealed theology (Latin: *theologia revelata*). Cognition of God "from revelation" (*CPR*, A631/B659). In the first *Critique*, Kant says nothing about revealed theology beyond mere definition. This silence may have to do with political censorship: as a philosopher, he was not allowed to publish in writing any criticism of Christian theology. Yet we also need to recognize that this silence is entirely consistent with his critique of rational theology. His express intention is to critique human reason, not faith; and his intention in the critique of human reason, as he explicitly states in the preface to the second edition, is "to deny knowledge in order to make room for faith" (*CPR*, Bxxx). Kant might well have tailored to political expectations, but we must not forget how he identifies the assumption of the limitless powers of human reason in the "dogmatism of metaphysics" as the "true source of all unbelief conflicting with morality" (*CPR*, Bxxx). There is, aside from political motives, this important philosophical reason why Kant is not interested in pursuing revealed theology in his first *Critique*. In *Religion within the Bounds of Bare Reason*, revealed theology is given a prominent place. For pure rational religion to be at all possible, naked human reason must be cloaked with revelation. See **knowledge.** Compare **natural theology; transcendental theology.**

science *(Wissenschaft).* A coherent system of knowledge consisting of synthetic *a priori* judgments on a particular family of objects. Kant restricts science to the theoretical use of reason, in which *knowledge (Wissen)* consists of synthetic *a priori* judgments produced by the faculty of the understanding. The higher faculty of reason synthesizes such judgments to form coherent systems of knowledge. While contemporary readers may be accustomed to the distinction between theoretical and empirical sciences, *science* is, for Kant, by definition theoretical. Yet a science can be pure (nonempirical) or empirical. Pure sciences involve what Hume calls the "relations of ideas" that are "discoverable by the mere operation of thought" (*Enquiry concerning Human Understanding*, 28). Even Hume acknowledges the scientific status of pure sciences such as geometry, algebra, and arithmetic. Kant, however, was the first philosopher to think of the synthetic *a priori* criterion for theoretical knowledge, and so he was also the first to demonstrate that the pure sciences consist of synthetic *a priori* judgments. This criterion allows him to demonstrate the possibility of empirical knowledge and sciences. As Kant sees it, Hume's failure to recognize the *a priori* character of the category of causality blinded him to the possibility of synthetic *a priori* judgments. The purity of the conceptual categories allows for the scientific status of our empirical studies of the physical world intuitable within the forms of space and time. According to mainline interpretations of Kant, metaphysical ideas, such as God, the world, the soul, freedom, and immortality, are transcendent to space and time, and so they cannot be objects of scientific inquiry. Note, however, that Kant's synthetic *a priori* criterion and his restriction of science to the theoretical use of reason also exclude the scientific status of academic disciplines such as biology. See **theoretical reason.**

sensation *(Empfindung)*. A cognitive mechanism within the faculty of sensibility. When an external object appears to our senses, we intuit it through sensation. Empirical intuition as such is to be distinguished from sensation, in that sensations are directed toward the mind, rather than the object, while intuitions refer to objects. More precisely, a sensation consists in the effect (*Wirkung*) of an object on our cognitive capacity for representations. Sensation as such is what makes sensibility an overall passive faculty, despite its act of intuition. That is, empirical intuition arises only as a response mechanism to sensation. See **appearance.**

sensibility. The cognitive faculty responsible for the passive reception of empirical objects by the mind through sensation and intuition. Sensibility is one of the primary cognitive faculties that Kant identifies. It works closely with the faculty of understanding. Sensibility represents to our minds the objects that appear to our senses. The representation of an object that we receive through sensibility is not the thing in itself, the ontological substance of the object, which the ancient Greeks and early-modern rationalists thought to be intelligible (such as the substance of wax in Descartes's argument). Sensibility represents to us the object as it appears to our senses. What is given to the mind through sensibility, then, is not the ontological substance of the object, but rather its appearance.

sensible intuition. A type of intuition that requires the existence of an object that produces an *effect* (*Wirkung*) on our capacity to represent: we cannot intuitively represent an object *ex nihilo*. Kant is emphatic that human intuition qua creaturely intuition can only be sensible. We cannot intellectually intuit objects without sensibility, which presupposes sensation. That is, we cannot represent objects immediately with the intellect. The only intellect that does not require sensibility in intuiting objects is that of God. Compare **empirical intuition; intellectual intuition; pure intuition.**

space and time. According to the doctrine of transcendental idealism, the very forms of the human intuition that make our experience of appearances possible. Space and time are, as such, not determinations of things in themselves that can remain when they are abstracted from the subjective conditions of human cognition. Kant thus speaks of the transcendental ideality of space and time, which means that they become "nothing as soon as we leave out the condition of the possibility of all experience, and take [them] as something that [grounds] the things in themselves" (*CPR*, A28/B44). Kant emphasizes that the transcendental ideality of space and time goes hand in hand with their empirical reality, that is, "objective validity," in our everyday understanding of the words (*CPR*, A27/B44). There are doubtless objective ways to measure extensions in space and durations in time to which we can all agree. What Kant means by the transcendental ideality and subjectivity of time and space is that they are the *a priori* preconditions of our intuition of all objects, and that as such they are unlike any object. Kant notices that we intuit objects in and through space and time, but that we do not really intuit space and time as objects. We, with space and time as sensible forms of reference, intuit objects that are in space and time. In this sense, space and time are the transcendental forms of our sensibility, and they are transcendentally ideal. Furthermore, this ideality entails that space and time are entirely *a priori* and pure (unadulterated with experience). Our representations of space and time precede our capability to sensibly represent objects in space. Because the representations of space and time precede any experience of spatiotemporal objects, they must be *a priori.*

sublime, the. The objective quality that induces a feeling of awe in the observer. In the third *Critique*, Kant offered an account of *the sublime* (*das Erhabene*) that elicited impassioned responses from the likes of Friedrich Schiller and later Romantics. While the beautiful triggers a positive feeling of pleasure, the sublime arouses a feeling of satisfaction that is "only negative": it is a "feeling of the deprivation of the freedom of the imagination by itself," characterized by "astonishment bordering on terror, the horror and the awesome shudder, which grip the spectator in viewing mountain ranges towering to the heavens, deep ravines and the raging torrents in them, deeply shadowed wastelands inducing melancholy reflection, etc." (*CPJ*, 151). The sublime as such "pleases immediately," albeit "through its resistance to the interest of the senses," whereas the beautiful only pleases without interest (*CPJ*, 150). In the presence of the sublime, we feel something greater than life, as it were—a cause that subjects us to "sacrifice" and willing "deprivation" (*CPJ*, 151). Kant distinguishes between the natural sublime and the moral sublime. Both the starry heavens above me and the moral law within me are sublime. Both occasion our rational faith in God: the "physical teleology" of nature "gives our theoretically reflecting power of judgment a sufficient basis for assuming the existence of an intelligent world-cause," while "we also find in ourselves . . . a moral teleology" that points us to God as the supreme moral agent (*CPJ*, 151). The main body of the third *Critique* is primarily preoccupied with the sublime in nature—such as the starry heavens (which pertains to the mathematical sublime, which overwhelms by quantity) and towering mountain ranges (the dynamical sublime, characterized by size and force). What Kant calls "the sublimity and inner dignity" of the moral law is discussed mainly in the final appendix, titled "Methodology of the Teleological Power of Judgment," which comprises a modified version of the central theological thesis stated in the second *Critique*. See **freedom; judgment, power of.**

substance. The actually existent essence of a thing. For Plato, for instance, universal forms without matter are the true substances underlying the cosmos—these forms are truly existent. Aristotle, on the other hand, defines *substance* as the combination of form and matter: forms cannot exist without matter. The Cartesian tradition assumes the dual reality of our minds and permanent substances perceived by our intellects. Locke remained in line with Descartes in this respect. Berkeley and Hume, however, challenged the assumption that our ideas of things correspond to substances outside our minds. Part and parcel of Kant's discussions of appearances and things in themselves is his notion of permanent substance. The "principle of permanent substance" is the first of Kant's three "Analogies of Experience" in the first *Critique*. Discussion of the three Analogies would involve some very advanced debates in Kant studies, not least because Kant's own presentation of the matter is fraught with gaps, if not inconsistencies (as some have alleged), in his argumentation. His textual treatments of the first Analogy in the two editions of the first *Critique* differ significantly also. Scholars generally agree that Kant is not speaking of an ontological substance, the thing in itself. Rather, he is referring to something that is permanent relative to changes in time, so that when we intuit an object in time, we have this permanent substance as our point of reference. In other words, permanent substance is a precondition or principle for temporal relations.

synthesis. Generally, the mental act of gathering and conjoining different representations, in order to represent them in one cognition. In the synthesis of manifold intuitions into a concept, the act is spontaneous. The power of imagination is the cognitive faculty responsible for the syntheses of representations. See **imagination, power of.** Compare **analysis.**

synthetic *a priori* judgments. Judgments of amplification— propositions in which the predicate contains information not already included in the subject—that combine *a priori* (nonempirical) concepts and/or ideas. Of all types of judgments, only synthetic *a priori* judgments are necessarily true, but do not lead us to knowledge of anything that we did not already know. Only synthetic *a priori* judgments—judgments of amplification that are nonempirical—give us knowledge of new information that is necessarily true. Human knowledge and science, in other words, hinge on the very possibility of synthetic *a priori* judgments. That synthetic *a priori* judgments are possible is, according to Kant, clearly indicated by the science of arithmetic. He gives the famous example of "7 + 5 = 12." One might be misled to think that this is merely an analytic judgment about the number "12" as a conceptual composite of "5" and "7." But, claims Kant, the definition of "7" is not contained within the definition of "5," while "+" and "=" are notions of which the definitions are not contained in numbers. Because every sign in this equation represents an *a priori* concept, the equation amounts to a synthetic *a priori* judgment. According to mainline interpretations, this criterion for *knowledge* (*Wissen*) and *science* (*Wissenschaft*) means that while physics is possible as a science, metaphysics is ruled out, and so are many other academic disciplines that we consider "scientific" today, including biology.

theology. In broadest terms, "cognition of the original being" that we call *God* (*CPR*, A631/B659). Kant distinguishes between several kinds of theology. See **natural theology; rational theology; revealed theology; transcendental theology.**

theoretical and practical cognitions. The two types of cognitions. A theoretical cognition is "that through which I cognize **what exists**"; a practical cognition is "that through which I represent **what ought to exist**" (*CPR*, A632/B660). Accordingly, the "theoretical use of reason is that through which I cognize *a priori* (as necessary) that something is; but the practical use is that through which it is cognized *a priori* what ought to happen" (*CPR*, A632/B660). See *a priori*; **practical reason; theoretical reason.**

theoretical reason. The use of the cognitive faculty of reason by which we come to judgments of *what is*, rather than *what we ought to affirm to be*. Recall that reason is a cognitive faculty. It is one faculty, rather than two. Theoretical reason and practical reason, then, are not two faculties, but distinct uses of the same faculty. The more precise phrasing, then, would be *theoretical and practical uses of reason*. The criterion for knowledge in the theoretical use of reason is synthetic *a priori* judgments. In the theoretical use of reason, ideas such as God, freedom, and immortality are only regulative principles. As such, they are only objects of faith. Compare **pure reason.**

thing in itself (*das Ding an sich*). The ontological substance of the object, which the ancient Greeks and early-modern rationalists thought to be intelligible (such as the substance of wax in Descartes's argument). According to Kant, human beings can experience only the appearances of external objects, but not things in themselves. Few, if any, scholars would contest the understanding that Kant acknowledges the existence of things in themselves. How he formulates the relations between things in themselves and their appearances, however, has been a subject of intense debates in the secondary literature. See **transcendental idealism.**

transcendental. An adjective describing the form of cognition that ascends above cognition itself, to "cognize *that* and *how* certain representations (intuitions or concepts) are applied entirely *a priori*, or are possible" (*CPR*, A56/B80 [italics added]). This definition shows that Kant takes the possibility of *a priori* intuitions and concepts—and, as it follows, synthetic *a priori* judgments—for granted. He does not ask *whether* they are possible. Rather, having transcendentally cognized *that* they are possible, he wants to find out *how*. Note that *transcendental* is not to be confused with *transcendent*. *Transcendent* qualifies objects of cognition; *transcendental* qualifies cognitions. The transcendent is beyond the reach of experience and thus unknowable, while the transcendental is independent of experience (i.e., *a priori*). All transcendental cognitions are *a priori*, but not all *a priori* cognitions are transcendental. In both editions of the first *Critique*, Kant gives a definition of *transcendental* early on in the introduction, when he "call[s] all cognition transcendental that is occupied not so much with objects but rather with our mode of cognition of objects insofar as this is to be possible *a priori*" (*CPR*, A11/B25). In this way, *transcendental* can modify a wide range of nouns. For example, Kant dedicates considerable length to the "transcendental deduction" of the categories; he discusses the "transcendental illusion" of metaphysical ideas; he ascribes a high degree of importance to transcendental theology while denying its scientific status. See **illusion; representation.**

transcendental idealism. Simply put, the doctrine that human beings can experience only the appearances of external objects, but not things in themselves. More precisely, human intuition can represent only appearances, while ontological constitutions of the things that we intuit are not identical with their appearances to us. Concomitantly, the doctrine states that space and time are not real objects external to our cognitive faculties, but rather the very forms of the human intuition that make our experience of appearances possible. Transcendental idealism has been central to debates on Kant's philosophy from the very inception of Kant studies. In Kant's own words, transcendental idealism holds that all appearances "are all together to be regarded as mere representations and not as things in themselves, and accordingly that space and time are only sensible forms of our intuition, but not determinations given for themselves or conditions of objects as things in themselves" (*CPR*, A369). Beyond this simple definition, scholarly opinions vary widely on how the doctrine is to be interpreted. The pivotal point in the debate is whether the thing in itself and its appearance are two different objects, or two aspects of the same object. Furthermore, if they are two aspects of the same object, are they so distinct from each other that we can practically treat them as two objects? All would agree that things in themselves are real. The point of contention is whether appearances are also real in the sense that they are somehow analogous to things in themselves. Beyond the problem of definition, scholars have also debated over the role of transcendental idealism in Kant's philosophy as a whole. Is this doctrine central and fundamental to Kant's system, or is it just part of a bigger picture? Is it an indispensable doctrine in this system, and is it compatible with Kant's philosophy as a whole? See Recommended Reading for contemporary scholarly voices on these questions. These debates aside, Kant's intentions are explicit: transcendental idealism is meant to safeguard empirical realism, the doctrine that objects of experience are real, against the threat of empirical idealism, the essentially Berkeleian doctrine that objects of experience are only ideas in the mind. Transcendental idealism is a formal idealism: it treats space and time as ideal forms with which we sensibly intuit the appearances of empirical objects. Transcendental realism treats the forms of space and time as objective things existing independently of our cognitive faculty of sensibility, and consequently interprets the appearances of external objects as things in themselves. According to Kant, this doctrine inevitably leads to empirical idealism. Only upon the supposition of the transcendental ideality of space and time (without denying their objective reality) can the reality of empirical objects be ascertained. In sum, then, transcendental idealism is intended to be at once a formal idealism and an empirical realism. It would thus be misleading to simplistically label Kant as an *idealist*. See **determination; representation.**

transcendental theology. Theology that "thinks its object . . . merely through pure reason, by means of sheer transcendental concepts" (*CPR*, A631/B659). Rational theology can be of two kinds: transcendental theology and natural theology. Here the term transcendental is in line with the definitions given below, with the additional implication and connotation that what is transcendental can be neither proved nor disproved by experience. Although rational theology in general cannot positively prove or disprove the existence of God, transcendental theology is easily capable of demonstrating the analytic inconsistencies of nontheistic positions. This is important for the theoretical use of reason, because without presupposing God's existence as a regulative principle, there can never be any unity or coherence in our systems of knowledge. See **concept; pure reason; theoretical reason.** Compare **revealed theology.**

transcendent-immanent distinction. The juxtaposition between the transcendent (that which transcends nature and spatio-temporality, and thus human cognition) and the immanent (that which is within nature and thus available to human cognition in and through space and time). Noetically (i.e., from the subjective perspective of the knower), *transcendent* qualifies principles beyond the boundaries of possible experience, while *immanent* describes principles that lie within these boundaries. Ontically (referring to the object itself), the transcendent "pertains to nature so far as its cognition can be applied in experience (*in concreto*)," and the immanent "to that connection of the objects of experience which surpasses all experience" (*CPR*, A846/B87). The ontic aspect of the transcendent-immanent distinction has sometimes been neglected in the literature, but the text here clearly shows that this distinction is not merely concerned with the theory of knowledge. Some things transcend our knowledge because they transcend nature. This distinction thus carries a manifestly metaphysical dimension.

understanding. The active cognitive faculty responsible for the production of knowledge through concepts. This is a primary faculty of cognition that Kant identifies. It works closely with the faculty of sensibility. While sensibility is for the most part passive, understanding is an active faculty, in that it applies its primary representations, namely, rational concepts, to objects that are given to our minds by sensibility, so that we can make sense of sensible things. Kant uses this term as a German rendering of the Latin *intellectio*. Whereas rationalism generally holds that we cognize with our intellect and not our senses, Kant insists that this cognitive faculty on its own would be empty and futile. As the faculty that thinks, understanding needs sensibility to provide that which is thought by it. Conversely, without understanding, sensibility would be fruitless, for all its representations would be blind and meaningless. As Kant famously puts it, "Thoughts without content are empty, intuitions without concepts are blind" (*CPR*, A51/B76). See **intuition**.

BIBLIOGRAPHY

Primary Sources by Immanuel Kant

Bemerkungen in den Beobachtungen über das Gefühl des Schönen und Erhabenen. Edited by Marie Rischmüller. Hamburg: Felix Meiner Verlag, 1991.

Critique of Practical Reason. Edited and translated by Mary Gregor. Cambridge: Cambridge University Press, 1997.

Critique of Pure Reason. Edited and translated by Paul Guyer and Allen Wood. Cambridge: Cambridge University Press, 2007.

Critique of the Power of Judgment. Edited by Paul Guyer. Translated by Paul Guyer and Eric Matthews. Cambridge: Cambridge University Press, 2000.

Groundwork of the Metaphysics of Morals. Edited and translated by Mary Gregor and Christine Korsgaard. Cambridge: Cambridge University Press, 2012.

The Metaphysics of Morals. Edited and translated by Mary Gregor. Cambridge: Cambridge University Press, 1991.

Prolegomena to Any Future Metaphysics. Edited and translated by

Gary Hatfield. Cambridge: Cambridge University Press, 2004.

Religion within the Bounds of Bare Reason. Translated by Werner S. Pluhar. Indianapolis: Hackett, 2009.

Primary Sources by Confessional Reformed Theologians

Bavinck, Herman. *Philosophy of Revelation.* Edited by Cory Brock and Nathaniel Gray Sutanto. Peabody, MA: Hendrickson, 2019.

———. *Reformed Dogmatics.* Edited by John Bolt. Translated by John Vriend. 4 vols. Grand Rapids: Baker, 2003–8.

Calvin, John. *Institutes of the Christian Religion.* Edited by John T. McNeill. Translated by Ford Lewis Battles. 2 vols. Philadelphia: Westminster Press, 1960.

Dooyeweerd, Herman. *A New Critique of Theoretical Thought.* 2 vols. New York: Paideia Press, 2016.

Hodge, Charles. *Systematic Theology.* 3 vols. Grand Rapids: Eerdmans, 1989.

Kuyper, Abraham. *Encyclopedia of Sacred Theology: Its Principles.* New York: Scribner's, 1898.

Owen, John. *The Works of John Owen.* Edited by William Goold. 23 vols. Edinburgh: Banner of Truth, 1967.

Van Til, Cornelius. *An Introduction to Systematic Theology.* Phillipsburg, NJ: P&R Publishing, 2007.

Other Primary Sources

Altman, Matthew. *The Palgrave Kant Handbook.* London: Palgrave Macmillan, 2018.

Anselm of Canterbury. *St. Anselm: Basic Writings.* Chicago: Open Court, 1962.

Caygill, Howard. *A Kant Dictionary*. Oxford: Blackwell, 1995.

Hegel, Georg Wilhelm Friedrich. *Phenomenology of Spirit*. Edited by Terry Pinkard and Michael Baur. Translated by Michael Baur. Cambridge: Cambridge University Press, 2018.

———. *The Science of Logic*. Edited and translated by George di Giovanni. Cambridge: Cambridge University Press, 2010.

Hume, David. *An Enquiry concerning Human Understanding and Other Writings*. Edited by Stephen Buckle. Cambridge: Cambridge University Press, 2007.

Lewis, C. S. *The Abolition of Man*. New York: HarperCollins, 1974.

Locke, John. *An Essay concerning Human Understanding*. Indianapolis: Hackett, 1996.

Palmquist, Stephen. *Comprehensive Commentary on Kant's Religion within the Bounds of Bare Reason*. Oxford: Wiley-Blackwell, 2005.

Russell, Bertrand. *History of Western Philosophy*. London: Routledge, 2004.

Schelling, F. W. J. *Philosophical Inquiries into the Nature of Human Freedom*. Translated by James Gutmann. Chicago: Open Court, 2003.

Schleiermacher, Friedrich. *The Christian Faith*. Translated by H. R. Mackintosh and J. S. Stewart. London: T&T Clark, 1928.

Torrance, Thomas F. *Space, Time and Resurrection*. Edinburgh: T&T Clark, 1976.

Troeltsch, Ernst. *The Social Teachings of the Christian Churches*. Translated by Olive Wyon. 2 vols. Louisville: WJK, 1992.

Wolff, Christian. *Logic, or Rational Thoughts on the Powers of the Human Understanding; with Their Use and Application in the Knowledge and Search of Truth*. Translator anonymous. London: L. Hawes, W. Clarke, and R. Collins, 1770.

Secondary Literature

Allison, Henry. *Kant's Transcendental Idealism: An Interpretation and Defense*. New Haven, CT: Yale University Press, 2004.

Ameriks, Karl. *Interpreting Kant's* Critiques. Oxford: Oxford University Press, 2003.

———. *Kant and the Historical Turn: Philosophy as Critical Interpretation*. Oxford: Oxford University Press, 2006.

Berkhof, Louis. *Systematic Theology*. Edinburgh: Banner of Truth, 1958.

Brandt, James. *All Things New: Reform of Church and Society in Schleiermacher's Christian Ethics*. Louisville: Westminster John Knox, 2001.

Brock, Cory. "Orthodox Yet Modern: Herman Bavinck's Appropriation of Schleiermacher." PhD thesis, University of Edinburgh, 2018.

Brock, Cory, and Nathaniel Gray Sutanto. "Herman Bavinck's Reformed Eclecticism: On Catholicity, Consciousness, and Theological Epistemology." *Scottish Journal of Theology* 70, 3 (2017): 310–32.

Debes, Remy, ed. *Dignity: A History*. Oxford: Oxford University Press, 2017.

Eglinton, James. *Trinity and Organism: Towards a New Reading of Herman Bavinck's Organic Motif*. London: Bloomsbury, 2012.

Firestone, Chris L., and Stephen R. Palmquist, eds. *Kant and the New Philosophy of Religion*. Bloomington: University of Indiana Press, 2006.

Frame, John M. *Apologetics: A Justification of Christian Belief*. Phillipsburg, NJ: P&R Publishing, 2015.

Grier, Michelle. *Kant's Doctrine of Transcendental Illusion*. Cambridge: Cambridge University Press, 2001.

Guyer, Paul, ed. *The Cambridge Companion to Kant's Critique of Pure Reason*. Cambridge: Cambridge University Press, 2010.

———. *Kant and the Claims of Knowledge*. Cambridge: Cambridge University Press, 1987.

———. *Kant's System of Nature and Freedom*. Oxford: Oxford University Press, 2005.

Hare, John. *The Moral Gap: Kantian Ethics, Human Limits, and God's Assistance*. Oxford: Oxford University Press, 1996.

Hector, Kevin. "Actualism and Incarnation: The High Christology of Friedrich Schleiermacher." *International Journal of Systematic Theology* 8, 3 (2006): 307–22.

Kuehn, Manfred. "Kant's Conception of 'Hume's Problem.'" *Journal of the History of Philosophy* 21, 2 (1983): 175–94.

McCormack, Bruce. *Orthodox and Modern: Studies in the Theology of Karl Barth*. Grand Rapids: Baker, 2008.

McCormack, Bruce, and Clifford Anderson, eds. *Karl Barth and American Evangelicalism*. Grand Rapids: Eerdmans, 2011.

McCrudden, Christopher, ed. *Understanding Human Dignity*. Oxford: Oxford University Press, 2013.

Palmquist, Stephen. *Kant's Critical Religion: Volume Two of Kant's System of Perspectives*. London: Routledge, 2000.

Peters, Julia. "Kant's *Gesinnung*." *Journal of the History of Philosophy* 56, 3 (2018): 497–518.

Rasmussen, Joel. *Between Irony and Witness: Kierkegaard's Poetics of Faith, Hope, and Love*. London: T&T Clark, 2005.

Rasmussen, Joel, Judith Wolfe, and Johannes Zachhuber, eds. *The Oxford Handbook of Nineteenth-Century Christian Thought*. Oxford: Oxford University Press, 2017.

Reinhold, Karl. *Letters on the Kantian Philosophy*. Edited by Karl Ameriks. Translated by James Hebbeier. Cambridge: Cambridge University Press, 2005.

Rosen, Michael. *Dignity: Its History and Meaning*. Cambridge, MA: Harvard University Press, 2014.

Scruton, Roger. *Kant*. Oxford: Oxford University Press, 1982.

Strawson, Peter. *The Bounds of Sense: An Essay on Kant's* Critique of Pure Reason. London: Routledge, 1975.

Van Til, Cornelius. *Christianity and Barthianism*. Philadelphia: Presbyterian and Reformed, 1964.

———. *The New Modernism: An Appraisal of the Theology of Barth and Brunner*. Philadelphia: Presbyterian and Reformed, 1946.

Wood, Allen. *Kant's Rational Theology*. Ithaca, NY: Cornell University Press, 1978.

RECOMMENDED READING

Reading Kant: A Strategy

There have been many different interpretations of Kant's philosophy since his own day. On one hand, one's interpretation is inevitably shaped by the strategy with which one initially approaches his texts. On the other hand, different reading strategies are informed by the respective interpretational models behind them.

I am a theologian by trade, and my academic training makes the deeply theological dimension of Kant's writings more recognizable to me than they might appear to nontheological readers. The strategy that I am proposing here, then, is aimed at highlighting the theological elements of Kant's texts. The reader should be cautioned, however, that this is intended only to establish an initial framework of interpretation that must be subjected to further (self-)correction. Once an initial understanding of Kant's philosophy is in place, the reader should come back to his writings again and again, so as to allow information in the written text to challenge various assumptions in the reader's interpretational framework.

My understanding is such that the *Critique of Pure Reason* sets the basic parameters for Kant's subsequent works, and so it would make sense for the reader to begin with this magnum opus. The text, however, is unusually difficult. Instead of reading through the entire work, then, I suggest that the reader approaching Kant for the first time begin by reading the prefaces to his two editions, with greater attention on the second. Then carefully read through the introduction. These sections are brief, but they make Kant's intent quite clear.

Skip the materials immediately following the introduction, namely, the "Transcendental Doctrine of Elements," in which the all-important doctrine of transcendental idealism is set forth, and then the "First Division of Transcendental Logic." Spanning nearly half the length of the entire opus, they serve to draw the epistemological boundaries of Kant's philosophy. Because these pages in the *Critique* are among the most difficult in the history of philosophy, and because interpreting them has given rise to some of the most central controversies in Kant studies, I suggest that the reader skip to the "Transcendental Doctrine of Method," found at the end of the work. It would be desirable for the reader to ascertain Kant's conclusions here before becoming entangled with his arguments in the first half of the *Critique*.

Having read the beginning and the end of the first *Critique*, the theological reader may find it beneficial to then turn to the "Second Division of Transcendental Logic." This division is on the "Transcendental Dialectic." The theologically equipped reader should be quite ready to follow the arguments in this division, because it deals primarily with metaphysical and theological topics.

Do not worry if the remaining pages of the first *Critique* appear esoteric upon first reading. Several readings and familiarity with debates in the secondary literature are usually required to gain a relatively firm grasp on this epistemological part of the *Critique*.

There are a number of inconsistencies in Kant's subsequent works. If the reader follows these works in chronological order, the critical corrections that Kant registers against himself in his later publications can be easily missed. I thus suggest that the reader begin with *Religion within the Bounds of Bare Reason*. Theological expressions pervade this work, which makes it relatively more accessible for the theologically equipped reader than Kant's other major publications. This opus sets forth his mature views on religion, morality, and metaphysics, and serves as a helpful key to accessing his later works, such as *The Metaphysics of Morals*. It also provides the reader with a framework with which premature views in, say, the second and third *Critiques* can be discerned, so that the reader may take these earlier works more charitably.

I am thankful that when I first read *Religion* as a doctoral student, Werner Pluhar's translation had just been published, with a very helpful introduction by Stephen Palmquist. This translation is now accompanied by a critical commentary that I consider indispensable for any reader who wishes to understand this pivotal work by Kant: Stephen Palmquist, *Comprehensive Commentary on Kant's Religion within the Bounds of Bare Reason* (Oxford: Wiley-Blackwell, 2005).

There are a number of different English editions and translations of Kant's major works. Consult the bibliography for the ones that I recommend. It is almost impossible to navigate through the labyrinth of his writings without a lexicon. I recommend Howard Caygill, *A Kant Dictionary* (Oxford: Blackwell, 1995). What is especially helpful about Caygill's work, in comparison to study tools of a similar nature, is that he offers intellectual-historical analyses of the backgrounds and subsequent developments of various Kantian terms.

For a comprehensive view of the landscape of contemporary Anglophone Kant studies, I recommend Matthew Altman, *The Palgrave Kant Handbook* (London: Palgrave Macmillan, 2018).

Secondary Literature: Transcendental Idealism and Beyond

Debates on how Kant's transcendental idealism is to be interpreted and what important function—if there is any—it serves in his overall philosophy are central to the literature on his thought. The brief sketch below is for the reader interested in this advanced topic in Kant studies. For a start, the reader may gain a big picture by browsing through Paul Guyer, ed., *The Cambridge Companion to Kant's Critique of Pure Reason* (Cambridge: Cambridge University Press, 2010). The scholarship in this volume is quite up to date, and different voices—including those opposed to that of the editor—are relatively well represented.

Among the major participants in contemporary debates, some of whom are not included in the aforementioned volume, Paul Guyer is acknowledged for his focus on context, but his interpretations often tend to read into the text what is not there, or even distort passages in which plain textual meaning is available. One of his major contributions is Paul Guyer, *Kant and the Claims of Knowledge* (Cambridge: Cambridge University Press, 1987).

Henry Allison is known to be meticulously faithful to the text, but when certain passages present different exegetical options, his interpretational claims can often be better demonstrated with information on the intellectual-historical or intellectual-biographical context. His magnum opus is Henry Allison, *Kant's Transcendental Idealism: An Interpretation and Defense* (New Haven, CT: Yale University Press, 2004). The 2004 revised and expanded edition represents his mature views. Michelle Grier's work on Kant's theory of reason has made an important contribution that pushed Allison to modify some of his views: Michelle Grier, *Kant's Doctrine of Transcendental Illusion* (Cambridge: Cambridge University Press, 2001).

Overall, I find Karl Ameriks's interpretation of Kant to be most comprehensive in its consideration of both text and context. He believes that some major differences between Allison and Guyer can be resolved. I recommend Karl Ameriks, *Interpreting Kant's* Critiques (Oxford: Oxford University Press, 2003). It is not his major output, but as a volume consisting of relatively shorter essays on Kant's three *Critiques*, it can provide the reader with a good overview of his insights.

Allen Wood is another authoritative Kant scholar whose commentaries on Kant are often referred to in recent debates on transcendental idealism, though he is not generally considered one of the combatants in this particular arena. The Christian reader may be especially interested in Allen Wood, *Kant's Rational Theology* (Ithaca, NY: Cornell University Press, 1978).

One promising trajectory that may overcome the impasse in contemporary debates on Kant's transcendental idealism is that set by Stephen Palmquist, which furthers some of Wood's insights. Palmquist's project is not on transcendental idealism. Instead, it is a proposal to move beyond transcendental idealism and interpret Kant's philosophy as a "System of Perspectives." Palmquist describes his theological reading as theocentric and metaphysical. Regrettably, theological and metaphysical readings of Kant have been unpopular for decades, and Palmquist's work has not yet received the level of scholarly attention that it deserves. This means that even though his interpretation is groundbreaking and promising, his insights have yet to be subjected to more scholarly scrutiny to give rise to a new paradigm. I recommend Stephen Palmquist, *Kant's Critical Religion: Volume Two of Kant's System of Perspectives* (London: Routledge, 2000).

Secondary Literature: Kant, Theology, and Religion

The aforementioned works by Allen Wood and Stephen Palmquist occupy center stage in contemporary discussions on the role of religion and theology in Kant's philosophy. An edited volume that gives the reader a helpful glimpse of these discussions is Chris Firestone and Stephen Palmquist, eds., *Kant and the New Philosophy of Religion* (Bloomington: University of Indiana Press, 2006).

My reliance on the insights of John Hare has been explicit throughout this book. I need not repeat the significance of his contributions here. Suffice it to add that in many passages, Hare offers helpful guides specifically intended for evangelical Christians. He not only corrects misunderstandings of Kant popular among evangelicals, but also points out particular topics on which evangelicals should not follow Kant. I have referenced John Hare, *The Moral Gap: Kantian Ethics, Human Limits, and God's Assistance* (Oxford: Oxford University Press, 1996), many times in this volume. A short piece that might be of interest to evangelicals in general and confessionally Reformed readers in particular is John Hare, "Karl Barth, American Evangelicals, and Kant," in *Karl Barth and American Evangelicalism*, ed. Bruce McCormack and Clifford Anderson (Grand Rapids: Eerdmans, 2011).

Another Reformed Response to (Neo-)Kantian Philosophy

A major Reformed thinker not covered in this volume is Herman Dooyeweerd. Van Tillian readers may disagree with Dooyeweerd on a number of points. Still, his system constitutes a powerful response to Kantian and neo-Kantian philosophies— which might not be exactly the same as Kant's philosophy. As

I suggested in this book, Kant's epistemology inevitably disintegrates human knowledge into bits and pieces. This is partly because, for him, what counts as *theoretical* knowledge must involve the categories of pure reason. The narrowness of the categories fails to account for the variety and unity of other spheres of human knowledge. Dooyeweerd's proposal of fifteen *modal aspects*—named with adjectives instead of nouns—is a robust description of that variety and unity. See Herman Dooyeweerd, *A New Critique of Theoretical Thought*, 2 vols. (New York: Paideia Press, 2016).

INDEX OF SCRIPTURE

INDEX OF SUBJECTS
AND NAMES

Shao Kai ("Alex") Tseng (DPhil, Oxford) is research professor in the Department of Philosophy at Zhejiang University, China. His research publications have covered areas including modern theology, Continental philosophy, Reformed orthodoxy, Song-Ming Confucianism, and philosophy of music. He is the author of *G. W. F. Hegel* (2018) and *Immanuel Kant* (2020) in the P&R Great Thinkers series, *Barth's Ontology of Sin and Grace: Variations on a Theme of Augustine* (2019), and *Karl Barth's Infralapsarian Theology: Origins and Development 1920–1953* (2016), and a contributor to the *Oxford Handbook of Nineteenth-Century Christian Thought* (2017) and *Blackwell Companion to Karl Barth* (forthcoming).